MENTAL EVALUATION OF THE DISABILITY CLAIMANT

MENTAL EVALUATION OF
THE DISABILITY CLAIMANT

By

FRANK O. VOLLE, Ph.D., ABPP

Clinical Practice
Chief Psychologist, Denver Mental Health Center, Inc.
Denver, Colorado
Formerly, Staff Psychologist
University of Colorado School of Medicine
Chief Psychologist, Denver General Hospital
Denver, Colorado

CHARLES C THOMAS • PUBLISHER
Springfield • Illinois • U.S.A.

Published and Distributed Throughout the World by

CHARLES C THOMAS • PUBLISHER

Bannerstone House

301-327 East Lawrence Avenue, Springfield, Illinois, U.S.A.

© 1975, by CHARLES C THOMAS • PUBLISHER

ISBN 0-398-03338-2

Library of Congress Catalog Card Number: 74-18257

Printed in the United States of America

BB-14

Library of Congress Cataloging in Publication Data

Volle Frank O
  Mental evaluation of the disability claimant.

  Bibliography: p.
  1. Mental illness—Diagnosis. 2. Brain damage—
Diagnosis. 3. Disability evaluation. I. Title.
[DNLM: 1. Disability evaluation. 2. Mental disorders
—Diagnosis. W925 V923m]
RC469.V6   616.8'9'075   74-18257
ISBN 0-398-03338-2

PREFACE

THIS BOOK DEALS with the mental evaluation of the disability patient. It can be read profitably by physicians of any speciality, by clinical psychologists. and by psychiatric social workers.

The book is intended to be a guide and reference for those who do disability evaluations, including medical specialists. Very few patients present themselves frankly as mentally disabled, even those who have suffered acute brain trauma. Instead they complain of various physical disorders and consequently are often referred to one medical specialist or another. They may arrive at the mental examiner's office only after the expenditure of considerable time and money.

The medical specialist will find herein practical suggestions and "how-to-do" techniques in mental evaluation to the extent that he can make an appropriate referral. The mental examiner will find a focus and emphasis of techniques he already knows that will help him do a better job of disability evaluation.

ACKNOWLEDGMENTS

THE ENCOURAGEMENT, support, and helpful suggestions of my wife, Delores Cushman Volle, enabled this book to become a reality.

Valuable assistance was provided by Jan Parkinson, under whose watchful eye the manuscript took form. Patricia Heron generously gave of her time to critically review the manuscript and make important contributions. Any faults that remain are entirely my own.

My teachers have been many along the way. Deserving special mention are Abraham Heller, and Warren S. Kennison and Joan Fleming, each of whom in their own fashion contributed to my becoming a better psychologist.

F.O.V.

CONTENTS

PART II
OUTLINES

PART III
SELECTED CASE HISTORIES

MENTAL EVALUATION OF THE DISABILITY CLAIMANT

PART I

Chapter 1

INTRODUCTION

THIS TEXT DEALS with the mental evaluation of the disability claimant. The author is a clinical psychologist, and consequently, the psychological examination is emphasized to some extent. However, the usefulness of this book is not limited to the psychologist, for a large part of the evaluation of the disability claimant involves the clinical interview and mental status exam (evaluation of symptoms and signs) which can be conducted by medical and nonmedical examiners alike.

What is required of a good disability examiner? Depending on the nature of the examination, professional specialty training will play a part. Naturally enough, certain patients are referred to medical specialists for neurological, orthopedic, and other medical examination. As regards the mental examination of the patient, however, professional specialty becomes less specific. With a certain amount of interest and training, medical specialists of various types as well as psychologists and social workers can undertake the mental examination of disabled people.

Certain personal qualifications must also exist in the makeup of a good disability examiner. Some examiners become irritated with disabled patients because of their frequent list of complaints, their "doctor-shopping," or their demanding attitude. This behavior is sometimes the result of not having been taken seriously by examiners.

First of all, the examiner would have respect for the people he examines. He should believe, until he has evidence to the contrary, that they are sincere in their belief that they are disabled; he should be interested in their welfare and concerned about their condition, and above all he would be free of a defensive need to assume an authoritarian stance or contemptuous attitude towards disabled patients because of their condition, economic, social, or racial status. Basically, we are speaking here of what we might call the character traits of the examiner.

Assuming the compatible character traits necessary to examine disabled patients, what is important next is attitude. A desirable attitude might be described as a spirit of investigation and inquiry, an open-mindedness about the patient's condition; clinical sensitivity and curiosity, an unwillingness to accept things at face value without further questioning.

Furthermore, the good examiner will also have an interest in the relationship between biology and psychology, and will have a belief that all behavior, verbal and otherwise, must be mediated through a physical organism that cannot be ignored. This view will be elaborated further in following chapters.

Chapter 2

THE DISABILITY PATIENT

DEFINITION

IT SEEMS advisable to define what we mean by the terms "disability patient" or "disability claimant." Essentially, a disability claimant is a wage earner who, for physical or mental reasons, believes that he is not capable of self-sustaining employment, temporarily or permanently. He may believe that he is totally or only partially disabled, and believes further that he is eligible for financial benefits provided by his company, Social Security, Workmen's Compensation, Veterans Administration, or those of a private insurance company.

Obviously this involves a large number of individuals. Through the Social Security Administration alone, in the fiscal year 1972–73 over 430 million dollars were paid in claims to over three million individuals (11). After cardiac disorders, the second most common diagnosis involved a mental disorder.

Workmen's Compensation and the Veterans Administration both provide benefits for a large number of individuals. Larger industries pay benefits to disabled employees, and many insurance companies sell disability insurance. In order to collect benefits, patients must all be examined by physicians in most cases, but in some "mental" cases, examination by a professional psychologist to determine eligibility for disability claims is required. The results are ordinarily adjudicated through a Federal or State agency, or the medical department of a private industry or insurance company.

The criterion for a judgment of "disabled" varies according to the funding agency involved. Social Security, for example, has the most rigorous and stringent definition. The patient must be incapable of any "substantial gainful activity" (40). This means the patient is not employable in any occupation to the degree that he could be self-sustaining financially.

Some insurance companies, on the other hand, use the criteria that the patient is no longer capable of pursuing the occupation in which he was employed at the time of disablement (29). This determination is ordinarily more easily made by the examiner than the broad, comprehensive one used by Social Security. For example, a professor of mathematics who suffers a cerebral vascular accident resulting in the loss of abstract thought may indeed be disabled in relation to his chosen occupation, but could possibly work at any number of occupations not requiring this higher level cognitive function.

This book is directed toward the measures that must be taken to arrive at the most rigorous judgment of disability, that is, that the patient be incapable of gainful employment. If less than that is required of the examiner, so much the easier is his charge.

THE REFERRAL QUESTION

The disability patient is ordinarily referred with specific referral questions in mind coming from the social agency, attorney, or other referring source. There may be a question of impairment or deterioration, a change in personality or lifestyle, perhaps a question of hypochondriasis or malingering, and all of these questions relate to the individual's claim that he is no longer capable of productive work. Although these referral questions orient the examiner to his task, they should not limit his exploration with the patient of possible other areas of difficulty (See Chapter 3).

Many times supplementary reports from physicians, schools, psychologists, or other agencies may be made available to the examiner when he sees the patient. All of this information should be read thoroughly. Not only should it be read, but it must be evaluated with a critical eye for determining whether previous examiners or reporters have overlooked important areas of investigation.

Supplementary information often includes contradictory opinions. In fact, not infrequently is this the basis for the referral to the examiner, in order to get more data on which to base an opinion regarding disability. The difference in opinion of previous examiners should be noted, with an eye particularly to explore these areas of discrepancy. Not infrequently the mental examiner is the last in a line of various medical and paramedical personnel who have seen the patient.

Information accompanying the referral often indicates a variety of diagnostic labels that have been attached to the patient. It is the examiner's job in such a case to resolve the diagnostic picture. To do so, he must "diagnose" the diagnostic problem, i.e. come to some understanding of why various examiners have seen the patient differently. In pondering this question, he will generate hypotheses that come into play even before he sees the patient.

THE FACTOR OF CHANGE

The nature of the examination, the direction taken by the examiner, the kinds of questions he asks, the areas of functioning that he explores with the patient, are all determined and relevant to one overriding general principle—the patient's claim that he is *no longer what he once was*. It is this change from past to present, the nature of the change, how it came about, and how we understand it, that is the essence of our evaluation. This change may be obvious or subtle, it may have been brought on by trauma, disease, or factors unknown to us, but for whatever reason there must be change and in fact rather marked change for us to consider that we are dealing with a disability. The change need not have necessarily been sudden but could be gradual and occupy a considerable length of time. Nevertheless, it must be present.

It may seem that we are overemphasizing this aspect of change. A moment's thought will tell us otherwise if we consider the purpose of our examination. We are evaluating a patient who, at one time or another, was capable of self-sustaining employment, but who now claims that he is no longer capable.

That he is saying "I have changed" is obvious. It is our job to determine how, why, and to what degree, and to accurately diagnose his existing condition by way of contrast to his previous condition.

An individual who is not changed, in the sense of his capacity for employment, is not "disabled" in the sense we have been using the term here. If he has suffered a long-term, chronic condition that has been with him throughout his years of employment, and he is no different now from what he was all along, he is not "disabled" in our terms. True, he may be disabled in comparison with other people, but he is not disabled in comparison with himself at some previous time. It is this latter condition, that he may be disabled in comparison with himself from a previous state, that should be the guiding principle in our examination of the patient.

This principle may seem obvious to many readers. However, a surprising number of examiners see patients for a disability claim and come up with a diagnosis of their current condition without taking into account their previous condition. This is true of both signs and symptoms as well as the overall diagnosis. For example, the fact that a patient cannot currently do simple arithmetic or cannot accurately read the paper is of importance in light of his disability claim *only* if he once *could* do simple arithmetic and accurately read the paper. If he once could perform these intellectual functions, we are currently seeing a deterioration of functioning. If not, we cannot judge deterioration on that basis.

THE TYPICAL DISABILITY PATIENT

What is the picture of a "typical" disability claimant? Over 70 percent of approximately five hundred disability patients seen by the author originated from the lower socioeconomic and educational levels. It is interesting to speculate as to why this is the case, and there is no research known to the author that bears on this question. It seems reasonable to speculate that those in the upper socioeconomic and educational levels are able to function at perhaps 75 percent or 50 percent of their "normal" efficiency, and still remain employed in some capacity, whereas the same is not the case for the other group. The lower socioeconomic and educational level group are many times trained in only one particular skill, and when this skill has been lost through disability, they have little else to fall back on. By way of contrast, a corporation executive who has suffered a loss of functioning of some kind may be able to find employment as a bookkeeper or salesman.

In one sense—not a personal sense but an economic one—we may say that the loss of capacity to function in his previous employment is more profound and devastating to the individual in the lower socioeconomic and educational level. A man who has worked his entire life as an appliance repairman, and then suffers a traumatic head injury resulting in a brain syndrome making him incapable of pursuing his trade, has few alternative vocational opportunities. In addition, his motivation to turn to other forms of work may be less, because his self-esteem has been tied to his functioning as an efficient appliance repairman. Consequently, he experiences his loss of function as devastating, as well it might be to himself and his family. Whereas another man whose self-esteem is less dependent upon his work may be able to accept a lesser job, our appliance repairman may be psychologically incapable of working as a dishwasher.

In addition to coming from the lower socioeconomic and educational level, a significant number of patients referred for evaluation of disability come from minority groups. These two factors, the low education and the minority background, can create for the examiner certain problems that must be taken into account from the moment the patient walks in the office.

In the first place, the patient may have difficulty in expressing himself. This is particularly true if he comes from a bilingual background. The patient may have a fear or distrust of authority figures, such as "doctors" represent. Because his sense of self-esteem is lowered, he may feel that he is going to be "attacked" or criticized by the examiner as a suspected malingerer. Often he will tend to focus on physical symptoms and problems, even though these have been ruled out by medical examiners. He may do this because his self-esteem is low and he is embarrassed and humiliated by his loss of functioning.

Other patients may feel so desperate about getting their disability pension that they will be inclined to exaggerate symptoms and mislead the examiner, or cause the examiner to be suspicious of their motives. If the examiner seems a bit abrupt or impatient, the patient may never get around to telling him those symptoms that cause him the most anguish and embarrassment because of his fear of humiliation. These are the very symptoms that the examiner needs to know about to make an accurate diagnosis (See Chapter IV, section on "Mental Status Examination").

Not being atuned to the patient's feelings and defensiveness has caused some examiners to arrive at a hasty conclusion that the patient is malingering. The examiner may not necessarily spell it out in those terms in every case, but that conclusion is implicit in his report. To arrive at a conclusion that there is "nothing wrong" with the patient, however that may be stated, is to arrive at no conclusion at all and does not constitute an adequate examination. That conclusion does not take into account why the patient is in the office to begin with; why it is he feels that he has changed and is no longer capable of functioning, and what his motivation was in making a disability claim. Even if we conclude that the patient is "malingering" and so state, it is still incumbent upon us to understand why he is malingering now and not last year or the year before. An exploration of that question may lead to information that has not revealed itself previously.

An examiner must be willing to take time and to have the patience to work with this special group of people. If he is not willing to do this, he should not accept referrals for evaluation of disability claims, for to do so can result in an inadequate examination and an inaccurate diagnosis that can do gross harm to the patient.

Chapter 3

DIAGNOSTIC CONSIDERATIONS: CLASSIFICATION OF DISORDERS

CERTAIN DISORDERS APPEAR more frequently than others in the disability examiner's office. Some of these are commented on in the sections following, although the list is by no means inclusive of all possibilities.

Differential diagnosis is difficult to make in some cases, particularly where we see "soft signs" pointing one direction, then another. At times diagnoses overlap so that we end up with multiple diagnoses. For example, personality disorders are found in a significant number of these patients, but less often it is the major diagnosis for disability purposes, although present.

In the case of disability claimants, we generally find more severe disorders than the "garden variety" neuroses that appear in the waiting room of the mental health center or the private practitioner. Although unquestionably many neurotics suffer from loss of efficiency on the job as the result of their disorder, only the more severe neuroses become disabling to the point where the patient gives up work entirely and files for disability benefits.

Conversely, the fact of employment alone does not rule out the possibility of a severe mental disorder such as a psychosis, for it is a well-known fact that a vast number of severely mentally ill people are able to make a livelihood.

The important question for the disability examiner is to try to assess as best he can the state of the patient's mental health prior to his loss of capacity for employment, as well as assessing his current mental state and functioning level. The question the examiner must ask himself is "Why?"—that is, why does the patient apply for disability now rather than one year ago or five years

13

ago? It is the answer to this question in depth that makes up our diagnostic understanding of the patient. For example, if the patient has suffered from chronic schizophrenia for many years but nevertheless was able to engage in self-sustaining employment until recently, it is our charge as a disability examiner to understand how that change came about. We must further understand the effect of that change on the patient, what it implies in terms of his capacity for employment currently, as well as some evaluation of its reversability.

FUNCTIONAL DISORDERS

Psychoses

In the case of functional (presumed nonorganic) psychoses, we generally see schizophrenia, psychotic depression, and borderline states of both. Schizophrenia alone is the second most common diagnosis among all social security claimants, and the predominant "mental" diagnosis (13).

If we suspect psychotic depression in a particular patient, we look for possible precipitating factors in the home, on the job, or in his social relationships. We refer to the clinical interview where we obtained factual information about the patient. Has he suffered the loss of a relative or close friend through death recently? Does the timing of that event correlate with the beginning of difficulties that the patient experienced on the job? We may seek possible explanations for a depression in terms of the patient's physical condition, such as menopause, a surgical procedure, or a chronic disorder.

We wish to explore carefully the events that occurred on the patient's job around the time he began to lose functioning capacity. Was he demoted or promoted on the job? Was there a reorganization of personnel in his department? Was his work load increased or decreased? We look for possible correlating events in the home. Is the patient undergoing a divorce? Has he suffered a loss of sexual potency? Have his children grown up and left the home? This is the same kind of exploration that any good clinician would undertake in evaluating a patient, except in this case the focus is towards especially understanding the decline in working capacity.

In the case of schizophrenia, it is not enough for the examiner to simply state that he finds the patient to be schizophrenic. That disorder alone may not constitute sufficient evidence for disability. Again, the examiner is confronted with the task of understanding why it is that the patient feels he is no longer able to work. Perhaps he has been schizophrenic for twenty years, yet terminated or lost his job only a year ago. Diagnostically, our evaluation of the patient is not complete until we can take that fact into account. In the case of acute schizophrenia, we search for a precipitating factor in the various aspects of the patient's life, as we would with any other patient. We are especially interested in how his schizophernia is interfering with his performance on the job.

Traumatic Neuroses

Another type of patient sometimes seen by disability examiners are those who are suffering from a traumatic neurosis (26). Often these are patients who have suffered an injury on the job, accompanied by feeling of fear or terror. Sometimes these patients refer to the circumstances of their injury as "nightmarish." Even though they recover physically from the injury, they find themselves incapable of going back to work.

This is a psychological problem that is most treatable immediately after the injury, and becomes progressively less treatable as time goes on. Unfortunately, the disability examiner often sees the patient after the passing of considerable time. By the time he is in the examiner's office the patient has developed a certain amount of secondary gain from his illness, and has come to displace the anxiety centering around the traumatic event onto physical symptoms or external circumstances.

If, as the result of his examination, the examiner feels that he is dealing with a traumatic neurosis, in most cases psychotherapy is the treatment of choice. Certainly it should be tried before the patient is certified as disabled, for once that has occurred the chances are less of his making a psychological recovery unless he is highly motivated and determined to do otherwise.

Iatrogenic Disorders

Related to the handling of the traumatic neurosis are those patients whom we must frankly admit are suffering from an iatrogenic illness. In one sense, these may be the most tragic patients that we see, because we are inclined to think that with proper handling at some time in the past their present circumstances of disability could have been avoided.

Examples of this kind of patient include those who suffered a traumatic neurosis and did not receive treatment early enough to benefit, as well as those who, through misdiagnosis, have been led to believe that they are indeed disabled and consequently settled into a pattern of life that yielded them secondary gains that are now possibly too difficult to give up. Occasionally we see a patient who has been found "disabled" and is paid a disability pension from one agency, and is now applying for disability through our referral source. If in our judgment the patient is not "genuinely" disabled, the chances are slim that he will give up the assured income he already has in order to begin employment again, particularly if that income is adequate to live on.

Is this patient disabled then? In a sense he is—for the most unfortunate of reasons as far as the helping professions are concerned. It is a rare patient indeed who is sufficiently motivated to consider psychotherapy or a trial run at employment, because it will alter an established lifestyle and result in loss of steady income.

Personality Disorders

Another group of patients who may qualify as disabled are those who are grouped by some practitioners under the heading of "personality disorders." We do not refer here to simply the psychopathic or sociopathic personality, but also to those patients who have been diagnosed as immature personality, inadequate personality, passive-dependent personality, passive-aggressive personality, and certain borderline states. These are patients whom we would not consider psychotic or organically damaged, but who exhibit a lifelong pattern of borderline adjustment and borderline functioning.

The disability examiner, confronted with such a patient, may feel frustrated in his diagnostic understanding of what change has occurred in this patient resulting in his inability to continue employment. It may not be possible to discover a well-defined time of onset of symptoms, and it furthermore may not be possible to relate changes in the patient to internal or external circumstances. Rather, what we seem to be seeing is a gradual deterioration of functioning, or deterioration of motivation to function.

These are patients who might be described as "burned out," "tired," or who have paid into their company's pension fund for many years and have now arrived at the point, through a combination and accumulation of events and circumstances, where they are determined to get "what's coming to them." After evaluation, we may feel that such a patient is indeed disabled, but not on the basis of any well-defined illness.

These patients seem to show a depletion of energy and motivation, which can be assessed by inquiring about their daily habits, activities, interests, their manner of relating to other people, and observing their personal habits, their appearance, and their efforts to care for themselves. These kinds of behavioral observations, of course, are valuable with any patient, but in this group we may feel that such observations are the main basis on which we arrive at a judgment of disability.

Hypochondriasis

Hypochondriasis differs from psychophysiological disorders (following) in significant respects. Anxiety is not "bound" in hypochondriasis as it is in psychophysiologic disorders. The hypochondriac is palpably *anxious*, which is consciously focused on bodily functions. This syndrome has many obsessional features. Further, hypochondriacs are notably suggestable, and symptoms change, as it were, almost "before our eyes."

The anxiety represents a displacement of worry and concern

about other matters, largely unconscious to the patient. The patient is capable of expressing a range of emotions, but cannot isolate or identify the "real" source of his continual preoccupation and worry. Disability is reached only at the point where the patient's obsessive rumination interferes markedly with his capacity for significant gainful employment. Psychotherapy is the treatment of choice in that case.

PSYCHOPHYSIOLOGICAL DISORDERS

Another category, that of psychophysiologic reactions, involves demonstrable malfunction or structural alteration of an organ or organ system, presumably brought about by chronic exaggeration of the physiological expression of emotion (40). Suspected disorders of this type include asthma, peptic ulcer, and certain allergic reactions, among others. Diagnosis of this disorder requires that the mental examiner work in conjunction with a physician. If known organic causality is ruled out by examination and laboratory procedures, the door is left open for the possibility of a psychophysiologic reaction existing.

A note of caution is needed here. To quote an oft repeated phrase in scientific circles, "absence of evidence is not evidence of absence" (2). The presumption of an emotional basis to various physical complaints can be evidence of a frustrated or overworked physician at times, rather than a carefully arrived at diagnosis. Of course the mental examiner can err in the opposite direction; finding no significant mental pathology, he sends the patient back to his internist. Professional people do not easily tolerate not knowing!

From the standpoint of the mental examiner, consideration of a diagnosis of psychophysiological disorder as a basis for disability requires the patient demonstrate to a significant degree inhibition of appropriate and "normal" emotional expression, accompanied by a lack of awareness of the appropriateness of such expressions, and a relative lack of conscious anxiety. Only then can we postulate a possible damming up of the normal channels of expression that could result in structural change.

In this author's opinion, to "localize" certain emotions with certain disorders is risky, i.e. dependency = ulcer, etc. A more general theory of stress underlying psychophysiological reactions seems more scientifically palatable (63). Disability occurs when the organ malfunction reaches a point where the patient is no longer able to work due to pain, respiratory distress, or other debilitating organic symptoms. The treatment of choice is a combination of specific medical measures and psychotherapy.

ORGANIC DISORDERS

A large group, diagnostically, found among those patients referred for mental examination of disability claims are those patients with organic disorders (48). This includes not only brain syndromes, acute and chronic, but toxic, infectious, and metabolic disorders as well.

Generally speaking, these patients referred for mental examination do not exhibit the gross kinds of neurological disorders that would have prompted their referring physician or agency to send them to a neurologist in the first place. Rather, we are speaking here of the so-called "soft signs" found in minimal brain disorder, or even more severe central nervous system disorders that are not grossly apparent. These "soft signs" may not reveal themselves in the routine neurological examination, EEG, skull films, or brain scan. The only way to detect them may be through interviewing and/or psychological testing in some cases. Neurologists are well aware of this, and frequently make use of the services of clinical psychologists for this reason. A skillful and experienced clinician, however, is sophisticated in the art of interviewing and can often elicit the necessary information in that way.

The examiner working with disability patients should have some sophistication regarding the signs and symptoms of neurological disorders and minimal brain damage. If we suspect the patient of having such a disorder, we direct our interview questions to reveal relevant information.

The patient's previous occupation may furnish us with clues as to areas we wish to explore in our interview. This is particularly important in cases of suspected poisoning, including heavy metal poisoning such as lead and mercury. These disturbances have mental as well as physical symptoms, and in some cases may be revealed only mentally first.

Among the group of organic patients, we see those who are suffering from disturbances resulting from infectious processes in the body, and overindulgence in drugs and/or alcohol leading to toxic states.

Metabolic disorders, among them acute hepatic porphyria and lupus erythematosus, have accompanying "mental" symptoms that may be the only apparent evidence outside of laboratory examinations in the initial stages.

Nearly all disorders that originate within the central nervous system, such as disease processes, tumors, and epileptic disorders, have mental symptoms that may in some cases precede by months or even years the appearance of detectable neurological signs.

The organic disorders mentioned above by no means represent a comprehensive list of all of the disorders, organic in nature, that could be seen in the office, (73). It is probably too much to expect of any mental examiner to be familiar with all the possible symptoms and signs of organic disturbances that could occur among his patients. Nevertheless, nearly all organic disturbances have behavioral manifestations, and we must never lose sight that behavior is mediated through the central organizing processes (central nervous system) of the human organism.

An observable manifestation of the functioning of the central nervous system is that bit of behavior known as speech, and another observable piece of behavior is muscular functions such as manual dexterity and coordination. Through the medium of these expressions of behavior we come to some understanding, or at least make hypotheses, about the organic substrate known as the central nervous system. This is why it is important for us to evaluate mental functions (signs) such as memory, judgment, capacity for abstract thinking, attention, orientation, and the functioning of the sensory systems including sensory perceptions occurring in the absence of external stimuli such as hallucinations.

MENTAL DEFICIENCY

It is the author's experience that the majority of those who have become disabled and unable to work for "mental" reasons fall into the above categories. However, not infrequently the examiner is asked to evaluate other types of patients, such as the mentally retarded who may be applying for disability on the basis of a retired parent's eligibility. With many of these patients, an evaluation of intellectual functions, such as using an intelligence test, is the examiner's major contribution. That is not always the case however, because we may get indications from our evaluation of certain types of employment that the patient could engage in perhaps only on a limited basis, which we might want to recommend to the referring agency or source.

Of course, mentally retarded people have emotional problems as well, and possibly advice or suggestions of environmental manipulation to a responsible party could be helpful to the patient as well as contributing towards his productivity.

Some retarded patients have been employed, often in menial tasks, but now claim disability; the examiner's job is to discover the reason for the change. Did he become depressed because of the loss of a parent on whom he was dependent for support and encouragement? Perhaps referral for medication or counseling is called for, or environmental manipulation could increase his sense of security and again allow him to become a productive citizen.

Some communities provide sheltered workshops and opportunity for a meager income by providing services on contract to local industries which could involve something as simple as the patient counting fishhooks and putting them in a packet. Many of those patients we term retarded are capable of some employment under the right circumstances. Our job may be to suggest to the referring source what those circumstances are, or to refer the patients on to a social agency.

Chapter 4

THE EXAMINATION

T HE EXAMINATION consists essentially of two parts. The first part consists of exploration of symptoms which we term here the "Clinical Interview," and the second part involves eliciting signs which we term here the "Mental Status Examination" (67, 68). It is useful to the examiner to distinguish between symptoms and signs (14, 40). Symptoms involve the patient's self-reporting of his condition, these symptom being elicited by the examiner by mean of his questions to the patient.

Symptoms are elicited in exploring the patient's family and school history, his employment history, his lifestyle as well as his own perception of his medical history. In the exploration of of symptoms, the input from the examiner is largely limited to focusing questions regarding essential areas of the patient's life and requests for elaboration of answers. This process, as will be seen in the section below, is much more complex than simply asking the patient to state the nature of his problem. We must be certain that we thoroughly understand why the patient feels that he is no longer able to work, and that we obtain adequate historical material to give a contextual background to the patient's reporting.

Signs, on the other hand, may be likened to "tests." Signs lend themselves to quantitative evaluation and include testing the sensorium as well as possible psychological testing. Here we are interested in exploring the patient's affect, memory, cognitive functions, orientation, and contact with reality. Of course, signs may appear during our exploration of symptoms, and conversely.

THE CLINICAL INTERVIEW

Our examination of the patient begins from the moment we first see him. We note his appearance, whether he is neatly dressed or disheveled in appearance, and pay particular attention to his locomotion and gait as he enters the office, his affect as he greets the examiner, and note his apparent age in relation to his chronological age. Was he accompanied to the examination by someone else or did he arrive alone?

As the patient is seated, we make note of any spontaneous comments that he may make. Did he have trouble finding the office? Did he drive himself or did someone bring him? Is he able to use public transportation? The answers to these questions are relevant to the patient's social, psychological, and neurological functioning.

As the interview begins, it is worthwhile to explain to the patient in simple language the purpose of the examination. The examiner should make a particular effort to modify his own vocabulary so that it will be easily understood by the patient. Phrases such as "psychological tests" are often best avoided, because they can make the patient anxious. In most cases, the patient does not know what kind of a "doctor" he is seeing. He has been instructed by an agency that a further examination is needed and that he should proceed to the office of "Dr. X." Thus, it is advisable to make a reassuring statement to the patient very early in the examination to put him at ease. The following is an example of such an introduction: "We will be talking together today. There won't be a physical examination. The purpose of our meeting is to get some additional information about you so that Social Security (Workmen's Compensation, your attorney, your agency, etc.) can make a decision about your disability."

Certain factual identifying information can then be obtained. The patient's full name, address, birthdate, and current age. Note in particular any memory problem regarding age. We want to know the patient's marital status and history of previous marriages. Does he have children, what are their ages, and are the children living in the home or away from home? We ask about the patient's own parents, whether they are living or dead, the state of their health, their ages, and if deceased, date of death and reason for death. We wish to inquire in a like fashion about siblings of the patient. We ask where the patient was born and raised, and, if he moved about during his lifetime, the reason for the moves.

We want to inquire in particular about school history. How far did the patient go in school? If he withdrew from school, what was the reason? In school, did he have disabilities or problems with particular subjects such as reading or mathematics? What was his favorite subject in school, and in what subjects did he excel, if any?

This school history is particularly relevant to the patient's disability claim. For example, if the patient states that "math was my poorest subject" and he is currently having trouble with arithmetic, we would not view this as evidence of a major change. However, if the patient states that he "always did well in math" in school, and we find during our examination that simple arithmetic is extremely difficult for him, we would view this as evidence of a possible deterioration of functioning.

To illustrate further, many disability patients did not finish high school. It is important that we inquire at what grade level they quit school and the reason for their quitting. We should not accept too readily the common excuse "I had to quit to go to work." Many times this hides the fact that the student was failing, which is important to know in evaluating his current functioning.

Regarding school history, we need to inquire about further training in the area of previous employment. Did the patient go to vocational high school, have training in the Armed Forces, etc.? How did he learn the skills required in his previous employment, skills that he may now claim are no longer available to him?

Next, it is important to take a detailed history of the patient's work experience, beginning with his first employment. It is in this area that the patient is usually most eager to talk, because it is his inability to work that has brought him to the examination. In most cases he does not present this material in any coherent or organized fashion. He wants to tell you how he was unable to function on his last job, which of course is important information, but we need to know about previous employments.

It is often useful to direct the patient's attention to each type of employment he has had and get approximate dates of this employment. We want to thoroughly inquire as to the reasons for termination in each position. This is of critical importance for our diagnosis relative to the patient's claim of disability. It tells us whether the patient has been a chronically ineffectual employee, or whether, on the other hand, he is currently deteriorated in functioning from a previously higher level of functioning due to trauma or illness.

As stated earlier, the patient's claim of disability contains within it an implicit understanding that there has been some kind of a change in his life. He was once able to work, and now he is no longer able to work, i.e. he is "disabled." Our understanding of *why* he is no longer able to work, or *in what fashion* he is no longer able to work, is the essence of the disability examination.

After obtaining the history of previous employment, we then turn our attention to the patient's most recent (last) employment. We inquire as to why the patient left that position. Did he terminate voluntarily or was he discharged? Many patients have difficulty explaining why they felt they could not continue to work. Sometimes their explanations are vague: "My leg turned numb;" "There was too much pressure;" "I started getting mad;" "I just couldn't do it anymore." Thorough exploration of this requires careful questioning. Many times the answer must be deduced from various data and cannot be elicited from the patient directly.

Open-ended questions designed to stimulate further thought, fantasy, or speculation from the patient are often useful in this regard. This includes questions such as "What would it be like for you if you went back to work today?;" "What did you used to be able to do that you can no longer do?;" "Could you do that job if you were sitting down (standing up, alone, etc.)?"; "What do you mean you get too 'nervous'?" Here, the examiner must use his own creativity in framing questions designed to elicit the information he needs to know in order to accurately describe the patient's disability.

It is from our description of his disability that we proceed further in our examination to test the hypotheses as to *why* he is disabled. The more accurately we can describe the disability, the more relevant will be our hypotheses as to its cause, the more efficient our examination, the more accurate our diagnosis.

Following our evaluation of the patient's most recent employment, we then want to explore in depth the patient's current situation. To do so enlarges our total picture of the patient, and adds to our diagnostic understanding. We want to inquire as to how the patient now spends his day, since he is no longer employed. This may give us clues as to skills or capabilities that the patient has that relate to possible future employment if he were retrained or reoriented toward some other kind of work. It also gives us clues in regard to whether there has been a deterioration in his activities, interests, and personal habits. We ask how the patient spends his day; does he have hobbies and if so, what are they; does he have friends; does he go to church; has there been any change from how things "used to be." Does he do any kind of work at all, such as mow the lawn, housework, "tinker" with the car, etc.?

Again, in these areas of personal/social functioning, it is important to get a picture to contrast the present with the past for this patient. For example, if the patient has no friends, we ask if he "used to have friends." The same is true of hobbies and recreation. This information is vitally important in our diagnostic understanding of the patient. If the reason for that is not apparent, we should remind ourselves that the central fact of the disability determination is that the patient implicitly claims *what he once was he is no longer.* To understand how and why that came about is our charge as a disability examiner. If, after careful questioning and evaluation, we are able to find no contrast between past and present in regard to the patient's intellectual, social, emotional, and medical state, we must then entertain the question as to whether this patient is "really" disabled.

We next turn our attention in the interview to the taking of a medical history from the standpoint of the *patient's perception* of his medical history. To do so does not require that nonmedical examiners be physicians, because our interest here is in both the factual as well as subjective information that the patient can furnish us without requiring a high degree of medical sophistication on the examiner's part.

We note that a very large portion of disability patients have been examined by physicians prior to their referral for mental examination, but for a variety of reasons the physician's examination did not yield the essential information and diagnostic picture necessary to make a decision regarding the patient's disability claim. There is much information that the examiner can elicit that will enlarge the diagnostic picture, and may furthermore lead to referral to medical specialists who have not been consulted. Also, many physicians have not had the training and experience needed to undertake a comprehensive interview with a disability patient, and consequently may have overlooked certain important areas of questioning or information.

A common complaint of disability patients regarding physicians they have seen is that the doctor did not seem to have time, or take the time, that the patient felt he needed to explain himself. As stated in Chapter I, many disability patients seem to have difficulty expressing themselves. This can be true for a variety of reasons, such as neurological deficits, poor education, or confused thought processes. What the patient complains about to his physician as his "trouble" should not be accepted at face value by the physician. Sophistication in the art of interviewing and willingness to spend the necessary amount of time with the patient can elicit much information that does not immediately emerge in the interview.

We want to inquire as to whether the patient is currently taking any medications, and if so, what they are and what is his understanding of the purpose of them. We inquire as to who prescribed the medications and under what circumstances. We ask about the patient's state of health, whether he suffers any pain or malfunction in his body, and if so, why he believes that that is so. We ask if the patient had any accidents or blows to the head that have led to unconsciousness, and if so, under what circumstances. We ask about headaches and disorders of the sensory systems. We inquire as to whether the patient has ever had "fits or spells" or fainting, tingling, numbness, and lapses in memory. We ask about venereal diseases, sometimes expressed as "bad blood" among lower socioeconomic groups.

Any answers to these questions that seem vague or ill-defined should be pursued further until the examiner is satisfied. One condition, for example, that is often overlooked in a routine medical examination are the symtoms of temporal lobe epilepsy, often expressed only in the sensory systems and which are frequently difficult for the patient to describe (16). To elicit information relative to subtle neurological disturbances often requires a patient, empathetic examiner who generates a feeling of trust in the patient.

The information obtained from the medical history can be very important to the examiner and to the referring agency or person, and not infrequently leads to further consultation from medical examiners.

The clinical interview described above, in the experience of the author, takes from one to two hours to complete. By now, we should have generated several hypotheses regarding the patient's disability that we will undertake to test by means of a mental status examination and/or formal psychological tests. These hypotheses evolve out of the data we have gathered during the interview, and they direct our attention to obtaining more material relative to the patient's emotional state, intellectual functioning, organic deficit, etc.

At this point, we should have had a variety of "clues" that direct our attention to various possible diagnoses. Perhaps we postulate that the patient is schizophrenic, that he suffers from a chronic brain syndrome, that he is mentally retarded or possibly even is maligering. Whatever our hypotheses, they should relate themselves to the patient's claim that he is disabled and that he is no longer capable of self-sustaining employment.

THE MENTAL STATUS EXAMINATION

Both standardized and unstandarized tests are available for the examination of the disability claimant. Standardized tests, those most often administered by clinical psychologists, compare the patient on certain cognitive, perceptual, and affective indices with standardization groups that have been established through research (1). Many of these tests have certain quantitative aspects or "scores" that place the patient within the realm of "normal" or "abnormal" in a statistical sense.

A less standarized kind of test is one such as the "mental status" examination most often used by psychiatrists, which, although it may be less quantitative in its measures, nevertheless represents a valid kind of testing by means of which the patient's responses are "scored" in the examiner's mind with normative date he has built up partly through his own experience (68, 73). The author has made a practice of using a combination of both psychological tests as well as a modified mental status examination which hopefully combines some of the better features of both.

The answers to some of the questions we might ask on the mental status examination emerge during the clinical interview, eliminating the necessity of inquiring about these aspects during the mental status examination. These include aspects relative to the patient's general appearance, his flow of conversation and association of ideas, and any bizarre or morbid behavior that can be observed. We also make observations about the patient's intellectual capacities, such as his wealth of general information, his educational and cultural level, and his capacity to communicate verbally.

In a more formal sense, we normally like to test what is sometimes referred to as the patient's "sensorium," which includes investigation of possible disorders of memory, orientation, his affective state, his capacity for insight, and any special symptoms that we may elicit (68, 73).

The patient's orientation as to person, place, and time give us indications regarding the patient's contact with reality and possible confusion of orientation to the world. It is useful to ask the patient the current date, the city in which he lives, the address of the examiner's office, and the examiner's name.

Memory is tested by asking the patient the name of the President of the United States, the Governor of the State, and the Mayor of the City, as well as asking him to name some current events or recent happenings commented upon in daily newspapers or television. The examiner can name three objects in the room and five minutes later ask the patient to recall what they were. Remote memory can be tested by asking the patient to recite the alphabet, giving the address of his childhood home, the nature of his first employment, and related questions. The examiner is limited only by his imagination in devising questions.

In the case of the disability patient, we are especially interested in whether there has been any change in these cognitive functions. For example, we explore this by asking the patient if he has noticed any change in his memory, or his ability to do calculations, and other cognitive functions to be described. If there has been a change, we inquire as to when that came about, and as to the patient's impression whether the changes interfere with his capacity to work in any way.

It is of value to test the patient's concentration and attention through such means as asking the patient to subtract in reverse order from twenty by ones and the more difficult task of serial seven subtractions from 100. We note any confusion of thought, wandering of attention, or errors in subtraction. We refer this data to what we know of the patient's past history such as his performance in school in arithmetic and his use of arithmetic on his job. Asking the patient test questions of certain arithmetic functions involving addition and subtraction, multiplication and division, will supplement this information.

In addition to memory, concentration and attention, it is important to judge the patient's capacity to think on an abstract versus concrete level. One method of testing this is through asking the patient to give the meaning of various proverbs. Care must be taken, however, to evaluate whether the patient's response to the proverb was based on his capacity to think abstractly, or whether it might be a function simply of memory or intelligence. For example, many patients give an adequately abstract response to "A rolling stone gathers no moss." It is important to ask the patient whether the proverb is "new" or "old" for him. That is, the response may be coming from memory, rather than from his capacity to abstract. In giving a series of proverbs, I always ask the patient to identify the ones that are familiar and the ones that are unfamiliar. Responses to proverbs that are unfamiliar to the patient are our best test of abstract thinking.

However, this is true only within limits, for as the proverbs get more difficult to abstract, a loading of intelligence enters in (72). A proverb such as "One swallow does not make a summer" is a more difficult intellectual task to abstract than a proverb such as "A new broom sweeps clean."

Concrete thinking in response to proverbs is a symptom found in both brain syndrome and psychosis. Ordinarily there is a subtle difference in the response of the functionally psychotic, however. The response is inclined to be more personalized, with possible bizarre or morbid thought content. The organically damaged patient is more likely to simply rephrase the proverb or restate it in different words, entirely missing that it represents an analogy to a "real life" situation.

Similarities are likewise a test of abstract thinking, for to perceive the similarity between two seemingly dissimilar objects or concepts involves abstracting out a common quality. Again, intelligence enters in as the similarities become more difficult. Consequently, we must always take into account our estimate of the patient's overall intellectual ability, based on his school history and work experience, as well as the results of our formal intelligence test.

A "similarities" scale is provided on the Wechsler Adult Intelligence Scale which can be used for this purpose. The results of this subtest can then be compared with the patient's total score. If a patient is of average to below average intelligence, failure to identify the similarity between an insect and a plant is likely not based on a failure of abstraction capacity, but rather is a function of his overall intelligence.

We evaluate these results in the case of the disability claimant in the light of his previous employment and life experience. If the school and work history of the patient gives little indication that he has ever dealt with abstract concepts, evidence of a failure in abstracting ability at the time of our examination does not necessarily indicate evidence of loss of function, deterioration, or disabled thought processes. On the other hand, an executive secretary or previously successful shop supervisor who has lost the capacity to abstract may indeed be disabled.

Another area that we wish to investigate is the presence of hallucinations and delusions. We test for hallucinations by asking questions such as, "Do you ever see or hear things that aren't there?" or "Do you hear voices talking to you?" Diagnostically, it is important to differentiate between auditory and visual hallucinations. Visual hallucinations are more likely to be associated with toxic, metabolic, or organic brain disorders. They often represent distortions of reality rather than a creation of reality that is not there. The classic symptom of delirium tremens is an example, wherein the patient misinterprets the wallpaper design as insects. Auditory hallucinations, on the other hand, can be both functional as well as organic in origin.

Delusions represent persistent distortions and misinterpretations of reality. This can be tested by questions such as, "Do you often feel that people are against you?" or "Do you read secret meanings into what people say?". With the disability claimant, we are interested in knowing how long he has been suffering from such distortions of thought processes and sensory systems. When did these symptom begin? Has he "always" had them, did they disappear and reappear recently, when did they occur in relation to his termination of employment? Has the patient felt that his bosses "had it in for him"?

We ask about periods of anxiety and tension, moods of depression, insomnia, constipation, loss of weight, and suicidal thoughts.

Throughout the examination, we must be especially sensitive and empathetic to the patient's personal and life situation. We make a special effort to adjust our vocabulary to the patient's educational level, and we do whatever we can to avoid an authoritative stance with the patient. With disability claimants, we have to take into account their lowered sense of self-esteem and realize how crucially important this examination is for their future livelihood. If they are genuinely disabled, their only source of income may depend on the examiner's judgment, and patients are very much aware of this. Consequently, their anxiety is heightened and their feeling of vulnerability exacerbated.

The patient from a minority group is often particularly defensive, stemming from an underlying feeling of vulnerability and helplessness. "The man" is about to judge him and, based on his life experience, many minority group patients enter the examination expecting to get a "raw deal." They express this in a variety of ways. Some patients enter the examination in an angry mood, saying, "I've been to two doctors already, why did I have to come and see you?"

Some patients obviously exaggerate certain symptoms, thinking that this will be helpful to their cause, when in reality they have many "legitimate" reasons for being considered disabled. The examiner must not be fooled into thinking there is "nothing wrong" with the patient when he sees obvious exaggeration of certain symptoms. The symptoms the patient chooses to exaggerate may not be the relevant ones at all. Other very important symptoms and signs may be present but the patient, in his naivete or defensiveness, may not even mention them.

In fact, in this examiner's experience, in a high proportion of cases the patient may not enumerate or may refer only tangentially to symptoms that suggest the possibility of genuine disability.

Astonishingly enough, a significant proportion of patients make statements to the examiner that could not be more damaging to their claim of disability. These may be patients who are so confused as to the purpose of the examination that they could not "fake it" if they wanted to. Examiners have been misled by this show of apparent open "honesty" on the part of the patient. By ways of example, some patients will enter the examination and make statements to the effect that there is "nothing wrong" with them and it is only a matter of time until they get a new job. When asked why they are present for the examination, they may answer that they do not know, or they were "sent" by their welfare worker or agency. These are not necessarily mentally retarded patients. Another patient may state, "The only thing wrong is I can't walk as good as I used to," or "My left arm is a little weak," playing down the seriousness of what may be the symptoms of a chronic brain syndrome.

Psychological Testing

The employment of formal psychological tests is an excellent aid to the diagnostic evaluation of the patient as well as a means of testing hypotheses that were generated during the clinical interview and the prior mental status exam. This book is not intended to be a textbook on the administration, scoring and interpretation of psychological tests, however, the reader may refer to the bibliography for references in this regard (1) (66) (9).

The author employs a standard battery involving the Wechsler Adult Intelligence Scale (75), the Bender-Gestalt Visual Motor Test (6), the Trail Making Test from the Reitan Battery (59), the Wide Range Achievement Test (6), the Rorschach (30), and occasionally the Wechsler Memory Scale (76). Tests of personality dynamics such as the Thematic Apperception Test and the Sentence Completion Test are generally not as useful as the other tests mentioned above in arriving at a diagnosis of the patient for determination of disability. These latter tests may be more useful in understanding personality dynamics as an aid to psychotherapy.

The Wechsler Adult Intelligence Scale tests two major kinds of cognitive functioning, verbal and performance (74). It also yields a "full scale" score which roughly approximates an average of the two. Each major scale has within it certain subtests that presumably tap varied intellectual functions of a verbal or performance nature. For the disability claimant, it is often more useful to compare verbal versus performance functioning than it is to make use of the full scale score. This is particularly true in the case of organic disorders that are often sensitively revealed by the subtests.

Generally speaking, the verbal scale taps the patient's capacity to express himself in a variety of cognitive functions through the use of words. The performance scale, on the other hand, investigates the patient's capacity to go about being "intelligent" through the use of his hands, and can, if necessary, be administered in pantomime. The scores on these verbal and performance scales, as well as their respective subtests, can give us clues relative to what is troubling the disability patient, and can aid us in our diagnosis. Again, we compare the functioning on this test with other information we have about the patient, such as his school and work history.

If the patient's employment has been such that he has relied largely on the use of his hands in expressing his intelligence, a relatively low score on the verbal scale may not be particularly significant. This is especially true if the school history and socio-economic and educational background of the patient all suggest the possibility of limited verbal skills. In such a case, we may not attach particular importance to a below average verbal IQ, but we may attach particular importance to a low performance IQ.

The fact that the Wechsler Adult Intelligence Scale is divided into two major sections—verbal and performance—is especially useful in the case of those patients who have come from a bilingual background. In the southwestern United States, for example, some Mexican-Americans went to schools that were taught in the Spanish language. In many cases the language used in the home was Spanish, and the patient may not have been exposed to much English until his school years. Obviously, with such a patient we would rely more heavily on the results of the performance scale than the verbal scale in our evaluation of the patient's intelligence. This may seem so obvious that it does not need to be stated, but more than one examiner has diagnosed a patient from this subculture as mentally retarded on the basis of a verbal IQ score.

Inspection of each subtest score on both the verbal and performance scale is useful in evaluating both disability and future job potential. The cognitive functions tested by each individual subtest will not be elaborated here, but suffice it to say that if testing reveals a loss of recent memory, attention and concentration, or vocabulary in a particular patient who has depended upon these skills for his functioning, we have material of obvious diagnostic significance.

The Bender-Gestalt Visual Motor Test involves the patient reproducing with pencil and paper the *gestalt* or form of various geometric figures. The accuracy with which the patient is able to do this is an indication of his accuracy of visual perception, but other aspects of his mental functioning are revealed as well. These include, among others, eye-hand coordination, finger dexterity, and line quality which may reveal tremors that originate in the central nervous system. Distortions and rotations in the reproduction of the designs are of diagnostic significance particularly in regard to organic disorders.

The Trail Making Test from the Reitan Battery is made up of two parts, A and B. The patient's performance is timed on both parts, and a score is available for each one as well as for a combination of the two scores, all of which can be compared to normative data composed of standardization groups. Results of this test give information regarding attention and concentration, show capacity to "shift" attention from one task to another, and indicate tendencies toward perseveration of thought. These are congnitive functions especially vulnerable to various kinds of brain disorders and disease(58).

For the disability claimant, use of an academic achievement test such as the Wide Range is especially important. This not only gives us some basis for comparison of reading and arithmetic with previous school and work history, but also gives us some idea as to the patient's current functioning level in these necessary skills which are practically mandatory for any kind of employment. The academic achievement test is an aid to the examiner in making suggestions to the referring person or agency as to what kind of work the patient may be able to do even if he is partially disabled.

The author has found the Rorschach Test to be especially useful in the determination of disability. It yields both quantitative as well as qualitative results relevant to the patient's personality organization and cognitive functioning. It is sensitive both to functional psychosis and impending psychotic disorders, as well as to organic disturbances. Neurotic disorders are revealed as well, although commonly they are not as relevant in the case of the disability claimant unless they are severe. From the Rorschach we also can get indications regarding the patient's lifestyle, which reflects on the so-called "character disorders."

The literature on the Rorschach is quite extensive, and the interested reader is referred to the bibliography in that regard (30). However, certain comments are in order.

Overt psychosis, and impending psychotic processes that have not yet become overtly manifest, are relatively easy to detect. These responses are often bizarre and morbid in nature, highly personalized, and show little regard for the formal properties and the cognitive challenge of the inkblot. Disorders of mood are often relatively easy to detect as well.

Many examiners are not as atuned to the more subtle indicators of organic brain syndromes which are also available in Rorschach responses (7, 51). The high incidence of organic brain syndrome among disability patients makes this test especially useful in the determination of disability (66, 9). Good indicators of organic disorders observed by the author include a low total response level, intellectual impotence and perplexity (expressed by statements such as, "I don't know what that could be," or "You got me there, Doctor, what is it,"), concrete thinking ("This is blood, isn't it?"), pure color responses, perseveration of response from one card to the next, and excessive use of white space.

The Rorschach record of the brain damaged patient is often similar in some respects to that of the mentally retarded patient, and this differential diagnosis is made on the basis of other information such as intelligence test scores, work history, and school history.

The Wechsler Memory Scale is an easily administered test of memory functions requiring relatively little time of the examiner. It consists of seven subtests labeled Personal and Current Information, Orientation, Mental Control, Logical Memory, Memory Span, Visual Reproduction, and Associate Learning. A Memory Quotient (MQ) is obtained which correlates with and directly compares to the patient's Wechsler Intelligence Quotient. This relationship to the intelligence quotient is important because it permits "comparison of the subject's memory impairment with his loss in other intellectual functions" (76). Futhermore, means and standard deviations of scores of the various subtests are available, and scores on these subtests can then be compared with each other.

The Associate Learning test of the Wechsler Memory Scale

for example, is useful in studying retention of recently learned material and was developed by Wechsler in his study of the retention defect in Korsakov's psychosis.

In general, psychological testing adds a useful dimension to the evaluation of the disability claimant. It is certainly not the only way to examine such patients, and it must be recognized that one of the major values of psychological testing is that it is a time-saving device. The skillful examiner, given enough time and interest, can make the same kinds of judgments about patients through interviewing as are yielded through psychological testing.

Those unfamiliar with psychological testing often tend to attribute to psychological tests certain almost magical qualities that yield "the answer" in a diagnostic evaluation. The tests can be only as good as the clinician who administers and interprets them. Furthermore, they should not take the place of a thorough clinical interview and examination, but rather should supplement and enhance the examination of the patient.

Some examiners who use psychological tests are inclined to rely on them exclusively, thus denying themselves the opportunity for the rich and varied material that can be yielded through a careful exploration of the patient's history and current functioning status.

Chapter 5

FURTHER CONSIDERATIONS

FURTHER INTERVIEWING WITH PATIENT

A DDITIONAL QUESTIONS and hypotheses may be generated from the examination that need to be checked out with the patient. These arise from clues that the sensitive clinician has responded to during the examination. Generally, they have to do with enlarging our diagnostic understanding of what has happened to the patient that has contributed to his disability. These questions, for example, may have to do with certain neurological or "soft signs" of possible brain dysfunction that might be clarified by judicious questioning (31).

Areas previously reviewed in the medical history-taking may need to be enlarged. Hints as to malfunction in the sensory systems may emerge as a result of the clinician's study of the material. Has the patient experienced any problems with vision, hearing, strange or unusal sensations, awkwardness or clumsiness, or incoordination? The nature of the questions will be dictated by clues that have arisen throughout the examination.

Functional disorders may suggest themselves as well. A hidden paranoia may be present. This might be suggested, for example, by Rorschach indicators of such a disorder. Does the patient feel that his employers and fellow-workers dislike him? Does he explain certain bodily sensations on the basis of occult or mystical influences? Has he become reclusive and avoided human contact?

INTERVIEWS WITH COLLATERALS

Interviews with collaterals such as relatives or friends of the patient are sometimes not only useful but absolutely necessary.

This is particularly true in the case of the mentally retarded patient, but often true in the case of brain syndromes as well. Many times the patient is simply incapable of remembering information that is necessary to the examiner to put together an adequate diagnostic picture. Other times, his attention or concentration may be so poor that he cannot focus on relevant questions, or circumstantial thinking frustrates the examiner in eliciting important information. It is not unusual for a spouse or other relative to accompany the more severely disabled patient to the examination. If they are not present in the waiting room after the exam, possibly they can be telephoned for further information. Of course, the patient's permission is asked to speak with collateral persons.

Many times a spouse or relative seems to be the only person who can give us a genuine "picture" of the patient. We ask for their impression of what is troubling the patient. Their response, although perhaps not medical in nature, may be very revealing. When did the patient begin to go "downhill"? Have they noticed anything about him that is strange or unusual? How does he spend his time, and how does he behave around the house? What occurred in his life around the time his work began to deteriorate? Was there a death in the family, did he have an accident, was he sick? How much alcohol has he been drinking? Have they observed what seems to be fainting spells, awkwardness; does he seems to forget appointments; is he irritable; how does he sleep?

HELPING THE DISABILITY CLAIMANT

Although the primary role of the examiner is one of a diagnostic evaluation of the patient in order that a judgment regarding disability can be made, he nevertheless has a professional obligation to the patient to be of help in his role as a "healer." In fact, his first obligation is always to the patient rather than to the referring source, and the patient should *learn* something from the examination.

The examiner's capacity to be genuinely helpful is a function of, first, his professional competence in arriving at an accurate diagnostic understanding of the patient. This is because whatever help he may have to offer is directly related to how well he understands the patient's needs.

It is, of course, enormously helpful to a patient who is genuinely disabled to have diagnosed that fact so that he can receive the financial assistance to which he is entitled. In many cases, this is the examiner's greatest contribution and its value should not be diminished in the mind of the examiner. On the other hand, if the "problem" is not one of genuine disability that qualifies for financial aid, the patient obviously *feels* he is disabled or he would not have put in a claim. (It is a moot question whether a patient who *feels* disabled is then in reality disabled.)

If in the examiner's judgment the patient is capable of self-sustaining employment, it behooves the examiner to recommend to the patient (as well as perhaps to the referring source) further steps that he might take in order to again become productive. This may involve vocational retraining, psychotherapy, or treatment by a physician.

Customarily, the request for examination from the referring source is oriented toward a "yes-or-no" evaluation of the question of disability. They have their job to do as concerns the disbursement of financial aid and the referral is in service of making that determination. They may or may not be oriented toward taking steps to help the patient in addition to the very real assistance they can give him financially. This is especially true if the patient does qualify for an allowable disability. In such a case, it may be of little value to make recommendations to the referring source as to how to help the patient, and it is incumbent upon the examiner to take the necessary steps.

For example, in the case of a suspected chronic brain syndrome or epileptic disorder, we will want to make referral to a neurologist. It may be possible that medication would be helpful. In the case of functional disorders of a neurotic or psychotic nature, referral for psychotherapy, hospitalization, medication evaluation or rehabilitation may be needed. The examiner may be called upon to do "social work" in the traditional sense, and assist the patient with planning, recommend a boarding house or halfway house situation, or some other type of environmental manipulation.

Certainly, recommendations to collaterals may be called for. The examiner may wish to advise a spouse, relative or friend as to how they can be of assistance to the patient. Parents of a mentally retarded patient may have made no plans for his living arrangements after they are deceased, and the examiner can be of real value in this regard.

The author has read reports of examinations wherein it is apparent that the patient was dismissed from the doctor's office following the examination with no further interaction with the doctor after the completion of the last test. The patient was told he could leave, and was none the wiser for the experience. Although ordinarily the patient does not pay for the examination himself, and the examiner's legal obligation is to the referring source, still his moral and ethical obligation remains to the patient.

It is not unusual—in fact it is common—for the patient to inquire after the examination as to whether he will be given a disability allowance. The examiner can explain to or remind the patient of the facts concerning that issue (ordinarily this is not his decision to make), but this does not leave him free of responsibility to be of some assistance to the patient if at all possible.

DETERMINATION OF PARTIAL DISABILITY

In the case of a patient that the examiner judges to be partially disabled, he should so state to the referring source and make recommendations to them and/or to the patient as to what rehabilitative efforts might be undertaken.

It may be that vocational training is called for, oriented toward development of skills and functions that remain intact in the patient. Perhaps a recommendation of vocational testing is in order, directed toward placement in a different kind of work. Although one patient may have suffered a loss of small-muscle function and eye/hand coordination, it may be that he is capable of using larger muscle groups in a different type of work. If complete self-sustaining employment is no longer possible through a change of jobs, the examiner may feel that under more ideal circumstances the patient is capable of working a few hours a day in a situation where there is less pressure.

It should be remembered that most patients *want* to work. They have suffered a loss of self-esteem as a result of their disability, and their self-image is often severely damaged. It would be difficult to overestimate the importance of a contribution we can make to patients if we can help them feel that they can again become productive members of society through guiding them in finding employment.

REEXAMINATION

Some patients present themselves with an acute rather than a chronic disability. In cases of this type, the examiner should recommend reexamination after a length of time. The length of time involved before the next examination is a matter of the examiner's judgment as to how soon the condition can be remedied or reconstituted.

It could be that the patient needs medical or psychological treatment of some sort, which can reverse the picture of an allowable disability. In the case of an acute head trauma, a certain length of time is often required for cognitive functions of memory and concentration to return. A disabling epileptic disorder may be brought under control through proper medication.

In any case, the examiner may feel that, although the patient is disabled currently, there is a good chance he can function at an optimal level again with proper remediation. The examiner should recommend this, both to the patient and to the referral source, and suggest to the referral source when he feels the patient should be reexamined in order to determine if an allowable dsability still exists.

MANAGEMENT OF FUNDS

If the patient is found to be so disabled that, in the examiner's opinion, he is not capable of managing the funds that he receives, it is important that the examiner state this in his report.

The examiner makes that recommendation if he has determined that the patient is lacking in good judgment, or that his capacity to handle numbers and number concepts is so impaired that he might become the victim of his own impulsiveness or of unscrupulous individuals.

In such a case, the examiner recommends to the referring source his opinion that the patient is not capable of handling funds that he may receive. The referral source may then decide to have the funds administered through a relative or a court-appointed administrator. This may not be to the patient's liking, but hopefully it will be in his best interests. Mentally retarded and the more severely brain damaged patient would be the most likely ones for whom we make such a recommendation.

PART II

OUTLINES

In this section are included a "Sample Outline for the Clinical Interview" and a "Sample Outline for Mental Status Examination" with sample questions included. The organization of this material represents only one possible way of proceeding. Other examiners may organize it differently to fit their own style of functioning.

Some general observations are in order. We must never lose sight of the patient's feelings and need for self-esteem in our efforts to get the answers to questions. This is true throughout the examination of course, but is especially true when our time may be limited in having opportunity to examine the patient, and in our own anxiety to do a thorough job we can sometimes forget that we are dealing with a person with low self-esteem who is probably already embarrassed about his condition. The information that we can get from the patient is a function in part of the patient's anxiety and sense of trust in the examiner. If we run roughshod over his feelings and cause him embarrassment and humiliation, our chances of getting information are reduced. Neither should we be so squeamish as to avoid direct questioning.

The sensitive clinician will be constantly assessing the patient' anxiety throughout the examination. He will note certain areas that the patient avoids, and he must try through gentle probing to explore these areas. Assisting him in his examination will be whatever sense of trust and alliance he has been able to build into the examination during the initial phase. He will have numerous opportunities from the moment he meets the patient to let the patient know of his genuine concern, his interest, his wish to understand as best he can what has happened to him, and his desire to be helpful in assisting the patient in expressing himself. The clinician communicates this in a variety of ways, not only through the use of words but through his attitude and demeanor as well. Even the physical setting in which he sees the patient contributes to building a sense of trust. If the room is noisy, if there is no genuine privacy, if nurses or other people come in and out of the office, if the examiner interrupts his interview to take telephone calls, he establishes barriers to sincere communication.

Questions from the examiner are not necessarily considered by the patient as being threatening. It is the manner in which the questions are asked and the examiner's capacity for empathy and sensitivity to the patient's situation that partly determine the patient's response. Knowing he is dealing with a person who has a lowered sense of self-esteem, he will make every effort to not embarrass him. If the patient's level of anxiety, and resistance to confiding information, are such that the examination cannot be completed in one visit, it then becomes necessary for the examiner to request additional time from his referral source. This is not a problem in the case of the company doctor or ward physician on an inpatient service, or perhaps even an agency examiner. It may be a problem, however, in the case of the private practitioner who sees patients on contract from referral agencies, and who ordinarily is allowed only a set amount of time to complete his examination. In a case like this, the private practitioner must request additional time rather than risk making a diagnostic judgment based on inadequate information.

SAMPLE OUTLINE FOR THE CLINICAL INTERVIEW

A. *Initial observations.*

Observations of the patient's appearance, dress, gait, and any spontaneous remarks. How did he get to the office? Did he come alone or was he accompanied by someone? Did he become lost, confused or disoriented in finding the office?

B. *Identifying data*

Name, address, birthdate, and current age. Note any memory problems with age or dates. Note the comparison between the patient's chronological age and apparent age.

C. *Marital history and immediate family*

Is the patient married? If not, has he ever been? Is this his first marriage? What were the reasons for terminating previous marriages? Age of spouse, number of children, age and status of children (living or dead, in home or out). Spouse and children in good health? Is spouse employed? Does patient pay alimony or support money?

D. *Family background*

Parents living or dead? Deceased when and how? Siblings, number, sex, and ages. Deceased for what reason? Employment status of siblings?

E. *School history*

Years of school and reason for termination? Special subject disabilities or abilities. Level of achievement—"did well," "did poorly"—grade average. Most disliked subject, best liked subject, hardest subject.

F. *Social history*

How does the patient spend his time since his disability? Inquire as to activities, friends, recreation, church or social group attendance, hobbies, and daily living habits. Investigate any changes in the above since disability. Does the patient receive any other financial aid? How has he managed financially since his unemployment? What is his actual income at this time? Has he been certified disabled by other examiners or agencies? If so, for how long has he been considered disabled?

G. *Work history*

Various employments and dates, beginning with the end of school. Reason for terminating each employment. Relations with employers and fellow employees.

H. *Most recent employment(s)*

Detailed investigation of patient's reasons for termination. Explore physical, social, and mental symptoms manifest at the time of termination of employment. Note concurrence in time with possible events in family or medical history. Inquire as to patient's reasons for feeling unable to work. What would it be like for him if he returned to work? What is it he used to be able to do that he can no longer do? What is his understanding of that?

I. *Medical history*

(Here we are interested in the patient's subjective impression of his symptoms and state of health as well as any factual information that he can give us.) Patient's perception of his state of health. Current medications, prescribed by whom for what reason? Intake of drugs not prescribed by a physician, including "street drugs." Alcohol consumption, previously and presently, how often, how much? Hospitalizations, surgical procedures, for what reason? Accidents, injuries, or diseases including syphillis and gonorrhea. Periods of unconsciousness, for how long and why? Disturbances and alterations in consciousness, including "fits or spells," seizures, and convulsions. Sensory phenomena: unusual sensations, tastes, smells, visual images, auditory alterations; sensitivity to light, heat, cold, hydration, or dehydration; dizziness, numbness, fainting spells, and *deja vu* phenomena. Problems with balance, awkwardness, clumsiness, and incoordination. Sinking sensations, abdominal pain, unexplainable anxiety or depression. Problems with visual and auditory acuity. Inquire about any changes in the above relative to the patient's termination of employment.

SAMPLE OUTLINE FOR MENTAL STATUS EXAMINATION

General Observations

The following is a listing of the areas we wish to test in our mental status examination. Among them are the central organizing processes, such as attention, concentration, memory, and other cognitive functions that result from a complex interaction between cortical and subcortical structures. In addition, we need information regarding the patient's mood and emotional state, his behavior, and the content of his thought.

The organization of this material and the procedure followed in doing a mental status examination will vary from examiner to examiner. There is certainly no one "right" way to proceed, but a thorough examination will cover these major areas. The sample questions suggested are by no means the only questions that can be asked. Examiners will wish to delete some of them and substitute questions of their own. It is not supposed that every question suggested here will be asked of every patient. Some of these questions will have already been asked and answers obtained during the clinical interview. Other questions, because of our clinical judgment about the patient's defensiveness, resistance, or low self-esteem, we will choose not to ask for fear of embarrassing or humiliating him. Naturally, our empathy and sensitivity to the patient will always be our guide as to how to proceed.

A. *Orientation as to person, place, and time*

    What is your full name?

    Where do you live?

    What is today's date?

    What day of the week is this?

    What is the address of my office?

    What is your understanding as to why you are here today?

B. *Memory*

    Do you have any problems with your memory? Tell me about it.

        1. Remote.

            Would you recite the alphabet, please?

Do you rember the name of your first grade teacher?

Where were you living then?

Do you have trouble remembering names of people you knew well in the past?

Who is the President of the United States?

Who was the President before him? And before him?

2. Recent.

If you have to buy three things at the store, would you write them down?

I am going to name three objects in the room, and ask you later to remember them. The three objects are _____, _____, _____.

Do you ever get lost when you go for a walk or a drive?

Tell me something current (recent) going on in the news the last few days.

C. *Attention, concentration, and arithmetical reasoning*

I would like for you to count backwards by ones from 20. Like 20–19–18 . . .

Now this is a little more difficult, but I think you can do it. Subtract 7 from 100 and give me the answer. Then subtract 7 from that and keep going down, like 100–93, etc. (If patient does not understand, examiner might substitute "take away" for "subtract.")

Next, I am going to give you some arithmetic problems to do in your head. You will find most of them easy.

How much is 15 + 11?

If you had $1.50 and spent 60¢, how much would you have left?

At 13¢ each, how much are four pencils?

A newsboy makes $32.00 in four weeks. How much does he make a week? (If these are too difficult, substitute simpler problems.)

D. *Abstract thinking*

1. Proverbs

I am going to say some "old sayings" that you sometimes hear people say, and you tell me what they mean. (After patient responds to each one, ask him if he ever heard it before or previously knew what it meant.)

A rolling stone gathers no moss.

Strike while the iron is hot.

A new broom sweeps clean.

The squeaky wheel gets the grease.

A bird in the hand is worth two in the bush.

2. Similarities

I am going to name two things that are alike or the same in some way. You tell me how they are similar (alike, the same).

orange — banana

coat — dress

table — chair

skillet — scissors

north — west

E. *Perceptions*

What do you believe other people think about you?

Do you often feel misunderstood or mistreated?

Does it sometimes seem that you are dreaming when you are awake?

Have you ever seen or heard something that wasn't there?

Do you ever hear voices talking to you? What do they say? Who are they?

Do you ever see visions of things or people? Under what circumstances? (Investigate visual and auditory hallucinations and distortions carefully to determine whether they are distortions of something that is there, or whether they are experienced in the absence of external stimuli. Also, investigate the circumstances under which they occur. Hallucinatory-like phenomena can occur under the influence of high fevers, drugs, alcohol, and other toxic and/or metabolic disturbances.)

Do you ever feel other people are putting thoughts into your head, or influencing your body?

F. *Mood*

Do you sleep well?

How is your appetite?

Do you often feel "blue" or "down in the dumps"?

Do you often feel excited and full of energy?

When you feel "down," what do you think about?

Do you ever think about killing yourself?

Have you made plans to kill yourself?

G. *Content of thought*

Do you worry about things? What sort of things?

What do you find yourself thinking about a good deal of the time?

Do you ever have thoughts that come into your mind that you don't understand?

Do you daydream much? What about?

Do you have ideas or thoughts that you can't get rid of?

H. *Behavior*

Do you seem to get along pretty well with other people?

How do people seem to react to you?

Are you a quiet sort of person, or do you talk a lot?

Is it hard for you to sit still?

How do you act when you feel upset?

Do you ever have trouble controlling yourself?

What do you do at those times?

PART III

SELECTED CASE HISTORIES

The following represent excerpts from reports of actual disability evaluations done by the author. The patients were referred by public agencies, attorneys representing individual clients or insurance companies, or physicians. Every effort was made to disguise the material to protect the identity of the patient.

Some excerpts are much longer than others. The amount of material included depends on the aspect or aspects of the evaluation the author wishes to illustrate. In some cases the material most relevant to the diagnosis evolved during the interview. In other cases the mental status exam or the psychological test results demonstrated the most relevant material.

As we know from clinical experience, diagnoses are seldom clear-cut. Signs and symptoms appear that point in one direction and then another. Our work is a continual process of hypothesis formulation and testing or rejecting of hypotheses. For the experienced clinician, much of this occurs subliminally, hardly with conscious awareness. Certain things add up "on balance," and we arrive at a diagnostic impression.

Such is the case also in the judgment of disability. No one sign or symptom determines the judgment. We weigh the psychological diagnosis against the requirements of the patient's job or even against the possibility of *any* substantial gainful employment, take into account the patient's history of employment, his efforts to compensate for his disorder, his interests and motivation, and arrive at a decision.

Several types of organic brain syndromes are illustrated. Each one emphasizes different aspects of this group of disorders. In applying for disability, all of these patients had been seen by one or more physicians, in the office or hospital, before being referred to the "mental" examiner. A definitive diagnosis had not been made, or multiple diagnoses confused the picture, as far as disability benefits were concerned.

Some of these cases illustrate the story of "the blind men and the elephant." Each specialist sees the patient from the aspect of his own vantage point. It is not that his diagnosis is "wrong," but that it is too limited in regard to disability.

All of these cases emphasize the importance of talking with the patient, of which the most important aspect is listening. Time and expense are saved when the medical specialist takes the time to do a more extensive interview and a mental status examination. These examination techniques are not the sole province of the psychiatrist or psychologist and can be learned by the interested general practitioner or medical specialist as well.

A CASE OF CHRONIC BRAIN SYNDROME, I

The following represents a type of patient seen very frequently in the disability examiner's office. The patient was a fifty-year-old white woman. The patient was examined by an internist who diagnosed hypertensive cardiovascular disease due to a central arterial hypertension, and possible diabetes mellitus. The internist noted that five years previous, the woman had suffered a cerebral vascular accident, but he felt that there were no residual sequelae according to the patient's report. The internist's letter to the insurance company indicated that he saw no justification for a diagnosis of disability, feeling that she could continue on her job with medication and follow-up.

The patient continued attempts to work for several weeks but was unproductive and reapplied for consideration of disability payments. Her records were reviewed by the medical department in her company, and she was referred to this examiner for mental evaluation.

The patient was employed as a legal secretary, a position she had held for the past fifteen years. When asked to describe in what way she was having difficulties on her job, she was vague. She stated, "Some days I don't feel very well. They think I might have a heart condition." When pressed as to whether there were any other reasons that she might be having difficulties on the job, she stated that she couldn't think of any and "it would be okay with me to work if I didn't get sick so often." She said that she had been taking her medication and that she had felt somewhat better. She went on to say, however, that her boss was displeased with her work lately and there had been a suggestion made that she might want to resign her job.

It was apparent why her internist did not pick up the possibility of a mental disorder with this patient, because she was both defensive about it as well as using a lot of unconscious denial. We certainly cannot accuse this patient of malingering, for she made no attempt to exaggerate or play up her disability. On the contrary, she seemed to give the impression that she could go to work almost anytime.

I asked her to describe for me the exact nature of her duties.

She stated that she spent a good deal of her time copying contracts from a master copy. When asked how this went for her she stated, "I have to put a ruler under the lines I'm trying to copy. Sometimes the line seems to slip down if I don't do that. Some days I waste quite a bit of paper because I find myself copying the wrong line." Lately she had been criticized by her boss for not finishing her work on time. When asked how long she had been having difficulty of this type, she stated evasively that she "didn't remember." When pressed further, she thought it might have been going on "several months." When asked if she had noticed any ill effects from her "stroke" several years ago, she replied that she had experienced some partial paralysis on the right side for about six weeks, but recovered from that with the aid of physiotherapy and went back to work. She knew of no other ill effects.

The patient had had two years of business college plus training as a legal secretary. She had few interests, hobbies, or recreation. She was unmarried and her main activity outside of the home seemed to be going to church. She belonged to no social or recreational groups, and when asked why not, she stated, "I don't feel very well lately."

MENTAL STATUS EXAM: Mental status examination revealed difficulties in both memory and concentration. Recent memory seemed impaired. When asked during the interview how she came to the examiner's office, she replied, "I took a streetcar," but there had been no streetcars in Denver for at least fifteen years. She was able to say the alphabet correctly, but when asked to count backwards from 20 by 1's, she made one omission in doing so. Serial 7's from 100 were completely impossible for her. Her series went as follows: "100–93– (long pause)–86– (laughs nervously)–(long pause)–I could have perhaps–(long pause)–I can't get it." At this point the patient began to weep and said, "I don't know what's wrong with me."

When asked the definition of common proverbs, she was able to abstract "When the cat's away, the mice will play," but when asked "A rolling stone gathers no moss," she replied, "I've heard of it–I don't know what to say." When asked the proverb, "Strike while the iron is hot," she replied, "Oh–I am pretty dumb

—(pause)—I don't understand things very well lately; I don't know how to explain these things." She was, however, able to respond correctly to common similarities.

She knew the names of the President, the Vice President, and the governor of the state. She could not remember the name of the mayor of the city. She correctly identified the examiner's name, the office address, and the current date.

When asked to do simple arithmetic calculations, she solved correctly the first three which involved addition and subtraction. However, when asked "How long would it take you to walk twenty miles if you walked at the rate of four miles an hour?," she replied, "Where are you walking to? I don't walk very much nowadays."

The patient admitted to no hallucinations or delusions. She denied feeling that people are talking about her or that others do not like her. When asked about her mood, she stated that it was "all right." When pressed further, however, she began to cry and stated that lately she had been feeling very "sad," particularly when she thought about her job. She had always enjoyed her work and did not understand why she was not able to do it as well as she once did. She did not entertain suicidal fantasies, her appetite was "okay," and she slept somewhat restlessly.

She denied any convulsions or seizures, tingling, numbness, but had occasionally experienced "ringing" in her ears, and had felt occasional dizziness which she said "passes" very quickly.

When asked about friends and associates, she stated that through her church work she used to belong to several organizations but that in the last few months she had not felt well enough to go. Lately she had been spending her time watching television, but she could only do this to a limited extent because it gave her a headache. She felt that there might be something wrong with her eyes or that she perhaps needed her glasses changed because occasionally things looked "out of line" on the TV set. She used to enjoy reading novels but no longer did so because she lost her place while reading. Embroidery was one of her hobbies, but she could no longer do that because of her visual difficulties. Lately she had taken up knitting.

To summarize the results of the mental status examination, we saw difficulties in memory, concentration, arithmetical reasoning, a difficulty with abstract thought, a mild to moderate amount of depression, and social isolation.

PSYCHOLOGICAL TESTING: Three psychological tests were administered. Bender-Gestalt reproductions indicated a mild to moderate visual-perceptual disturbance. Performance on the Trails Test, Parts A and B, was far overtime from that of normal subjects, falling well within the organic range.

Rorschach productions revealed no psychosis or impending psychotic process. However, we saw what appeared to be a severely organically damaged person. The record was characterized by moderate to severe intellectual impotence, perplexity, and failure to respond. Total number of responses to the ten cards was eight. To illustrate her intellectual impotence, note the following: Card II, "It doesn't look like anything (long pause) —it just doesn't seem to register anything to me—(pause)—just a blot—(laugh)." The patient responded, "It doesn't look like anything," to three other cards of the Rorschach series. Some vestige of her previous intellectual level was revealed in her one response to Card X, "Sort of like octopi—I guess that's the plural of octopus."

The administration of a formal intelligence test did not seem needed to establish a diagnosis, nor was the expense justifiable. It was quite apparent from the clinical interview and mental status material that we were seeing a rather severely disabled patient on the basis of a chronic brain syndrome, etiology uncertain. It may be that we were seeing the residual from her cerebral vascular accident of some years previous, or possibly she had suffered vascular difficulties since that time.

DIAGNOSTIC IMPRESSION: Chronic brain syndrome, moderate, etiology uncertain.

COMMENTS: Most certainly this patient was completely disabled as far as pursuing her previous occupation was concerned. It was possible she could be partially self-supporting at some repetitive task if she were allowed to proceed at her own rate and were given plenty of time to train on the job. This was assuming, of course, that she was physically capable of getting to and from work as far as her cardiovascular problem was concerned. This patient's life had centered around being successful on the job, and her apparent depression was reactive to her physical and mental disability.

It is possible that with vocational counseling and assistance in finding a different type of work, she could continue to be a productive person and financially self-sustaining. I recommend referral to a vocational testing and placement agency. Until she is retrained and placed on a new job, however, I believe she should be considered to be completely disabled.

A CASE OF CHRONIC BRAIN SYNDROME, II

This case illustrates the importance of mental status testing and sympathetic interviewing with a disability patient where the internist found the diagnosis to be equivocal, or there were a multiplicity of diagnoses, none of them clear-cut. This is not an unusual type of disability referral.

The patient was a thirty-seven-year-old white male. He was applying for disability funds from a public agency. Supplemental information accompanying the referral included a recent work-up in internal medicine done at a local hospital. The patient entered the hospital with low back pain as his primary symptom. In interviewing the patient, the internist elicited a history from three years previous of numbness of the entire left side, headaches behind the left ear for nine months, and stuttering speech for six weeks. Consequently, the internist requested a neuropsychiatric consultation, and the neuropsychiatrist diagnosed a probable conversion reaction but recommended further study.

An orthopedic consultant was called in, and he diagnosed a psychophysiological reaction—lower back syndrome. Since the diagnoses up to this point seemed to be going in the direction of a possible psychiatric problem, another psychiatrist was called in. He noted in his report that the patient had not worked for three years, that he was chronically anxious, and his diagnosis was passive-dependent personality, conversion reaction, and psychophysiological reaction with multiple physical complaints in the past.

Laboratory work-up was negative except for a slightly elevated cholesterol. Xrays of the thoracic and lumbar spine were negative, and those of the cervical spine revealed only minimal changes. Because of a possible history of hematura, a GU consultation was requested with no findings on cystoscopy or IVP.

The final diagnosis upon discharge from the hospital was "chronic anxiety reaction with hyperventilation syndrome," "psychophysiological musculoskeletal reaction, low back pain," and on discharge, therapy was primarily symptomatic, with the use of drugs and physiotherapy. An attempt was made to explain to the patient and his wife the nature of his illness. The patient was instructed in the use of a plastic bag for rebreathing to control the hyperventilation attacks. Regarding the disability, the patient was judged "status competent."

At the time of the disability examination, the patient was found to be a rather heavy-set man who looked older than his stated age. Throughout most of the examination he sat looking at the floor, and his speech was characterized by constant stammering. He had a passive-dependent attitude, occasionally weeping in a self-pitying fashion, but his tears also reflected some real depression.

He stated that approximately three years previously he was located in Florida and was a district sales manager for a large insurance company. He was very proud of that fact, and frequently stated that he "once made a lot of money." In a rather pathetic fashion he stated, "I'm getting better, I know I am, I'm going to be all right and make a lot of money again."

The patient was very difficult to interview. His thoughts wandered, he was circumstantial in his thinking, and it was impossible to get any dates from him regarding his history. Rather than admit he could not remember, he gave evasive answers.

Important information emerged only tangentially and in a rather incoherent fashion. In replying to a question about his previous employment, he stated that "something happened" on the job, and that one day he "blew up and told them all to go to hell." He went on to say that he did not know why he did that, and he wished now that he had not done it.

As can best be determined, after walking off his job, the patient spent the next three years at home and did not attempt further employment. His wife went to work at a sewing job in order to support the family. The patient had a personal physi-cian and apparently went to him more than one time. He stated that at one time he had an EEG examination in Florida but "there wasn't anything wrong with my brain." Presently the patient complained that he had back and shoulder pain, that he had "dizzy spells," and "terrible backaches, headaches, and blackout spells." It was difficult to get him to define the nature of these blackout spells, but apparently he does fall to the ·ground.

On mental status exam the patient demonstrated a pronounced difficulty in memory. He could not remember how long he had been married, except that he was married sometime in the month of February. He could not remember how long he went to high school, saying, "A short while—I think maybe two years —I don't know." Several times he wished that his wife were with him in the interview because she could answer questions that he could not remember.

The patient's speech was stammering, associations were loose, attention span was short, and he showed marked difficulty in following the examiner's questions. Illustration of the patient's flow of ideas follows:

Examiner: What kind of work do you do?

Patient: I used to be smart and I could sell real good. I was around over there—you know. I was gone from home. Gone, gone, gone all the time. I liked to sell.

Examiner: How many years did you sell?

Patient: Quite a few. A long time. I sold fruit as a kid. Then I got into insurance and made a lot of money.

Examiner: When did you stop work?

Patient: I still take care of the lawn. Do you like rabbits. I still got a whole bunch of rabbits. I take care of them, and a milk cow.

Examiner: Why don't you sell anymore?

Patient: I think I could. I'm gonna do it. I'm all right, I know I can do it. I made a lot of money. My speech is getting better. It's not so bad now, the speech therapist helped me some.

Pretty soon I'm going to get better. I was district manager and had a lot of money. I think my brains are all right because something else is wrong. I've got these pains in my back and in my head.

The patient was able to count backwards from 20, although in a halting fashion. In subtracting serial 7's from 100 he made several errors. He also showed no insight into his errors. His responses were as follows: "100–93–87–80–73–67–60–53–47–40–33–27–20–13–6, there, I got these right."

He was quite concrete in answering proverbs. To "When the cat's away, the mice will play," he replied "What does that mean? (Examiner: "What do you think?") "It's a funny joke, I think." To "Rolling stone gathers no moss," he replied, "Yes, then you never have nothing—I know that one." To "Strike while the iron is hot," he stated, "It's like hitting the desk." The patient then struck the desk several times while repeating the proverb out loud. The examiner asked if he could guess at the answer. The patient then perseverated and repeated "just guess" out loud several times. He could not seem to stop repeating the phrase, so the examiner stopped him and asked the meaning of the proverb. The patient then stated, "Strike, strike, I got that one."

In response to similarities, the patient got one correctly, but on the remainder could see no similarity. For example, cat and mouse he replied, "They aren't alike." To axe and saw the patient replied, "They are both long." and to north and west the patient replied, "North is looking that way, and west is down that way from the corner of the house."

The patient admitted to no hallucinations, auditory or visual. As best can be determined—because it was difficult to interview him—he did not suffer from delusional ideas. He did suffer from obsessive thoughts about getting back to work, thinking about it constantly. He tended to blame it on his back and made a point of saying, "It's not my brains."

Medical history was extremely difficult to elicit because of the patient's difficulty in remembering. He stated that twenty years previously he suffered a "heart attack" while in the service. Apparently he was hospitalized for a period of time in the service.

His discharge was a medical one. He had a tendency to suffer from various aches and pains, usually of the muscular-skeletal system, but in spite of that he apparently was able to continue working. He had a urinary tract infection at one time in Florida, which was treated by "pills." After quitting his job, his wife urged him to go to the family doctor, and it was at that time that he suffered numbness, headaches, and speech difficulties. An EEG was done with unknown results, except the patient's report that "there was nothing wrong with my brains." On his own, the patient went to a speech therapist to help him with his stuttering. The stuttering developed after he walked off the job. No further medical history was elicited. A history of alcohol consumption was denied.

When asked to do simple calculations, the patient proved himself to be intellectually impotent. When asked, "If you have $4 and $5 more, how much would you have?", he replied after a long pause, "I want to go back to work," and began to weep and wring his hands. With great feelings of inadequacy, he stated, "I was always very good in arithmetic." Upon further examination he was able to solve some very simple arithmetic problems, but he could not properly substract 14 from 50, $6.50 from $15.00, nor multiply $1.60 times 2. We must remember that this man was once a successful insurance salesman. He must have dealt with basic arithmetic problems continually in his career.

The patient's affect was characterized by a depressed mood. He wept several times throughout the interview, particularly when confronted with his inadquacies when asked to solve problems. He stated that he did not sleep well and took "sleeping pills," apparently prescribed for him by his family doctor. He denied constipation and his appetite seemed satisfactory. He was probably thirty to forty pounds overweight. He denied any weight loss in the last year.

To summarize the mental status up to this point, we see marked interference with the patient's memory, his associations were loose, his thinking was circumstantial, he had lost the capacity to think abstractly, he showed pronounced difficulty in calculations, and his mood was depressed.

Three psychological tests were administered. The patient's

reproduction of stimulus figures on the Bender-Gestalt demonstrated a marked visual-perceptual disorder. Some of his angles in the drawings were drawn in the opposite direction from what they should have been.

On the Trails Test, the patient's score was markedly overtime, well within the organic range.

The patient's response to Rorschach cards showed concrete thinking ("That *is* a hide, isn't it?"), intellectual impotence ("I just don't know—I can't think of it—I don't know—it's not anything—it looks like it might be a head up there, but it could be a tail, I just don't know"), perplexity ("Is that supposed to be something?"), and pronounced depression.

All of the psychological tests were markedly consistent with a diagnosis of chronic brain syndrome.

DIAGNOSTIC IMPRESSION: Interview material and mental status examination as well as psychological test results all demonstrated markedly the presence of a chronic brain syndrome, moderate to severe, etiology uncertain but possibly resulting from a CVA several years ago at the time he walked off his job.

COMMENTS: There is no question that this patient is disabled. There is a marked contrast betwen his present cognitive functioning and his previous functioning as district manager of an insurance company.

Considering the degree of intellectual impairment in this man, it is difficult to understand why his condition was not recognized by his physicians in the hospital. Perhaps his self-pitying attitude and dependency irritated his examiners and led them in the direction of a diagnosis of a functional disorder. He is not capable of managing his own funds. The patient was referred for neurological consultation to a private physician.

A CASE OF CHRONIC BRAIN SYNDROME, TRAUMATIC IN ORIGIN

This case was selected to illustrate the importance of the interview material in arriving at a judgment of disability. The patient was a thirty-six-year-old white female. She had been followed by a neurologist, and was also examined by a psychologist, neither of whom felt that she was disabled at the time of their examinations. She was applying for disability for the second time through a public agency.

Four years previously the patient was involved in an automobile accident. She was riding in the front seat on the right-hand side, and the automobile was struck by another, coming from the rider's side. The patient sustained serious head injuries as well as a broken pelvis. She was hospitalized for six weeks. The first two weeks she was comatose and fed IV. Upon regaining consciousness she was at first unable to speak. She suffered a hemiparesis on the right side as well as an incomplete third nerve palsy on the right.

Following hospitalization, she was referred for occupational therapy and was seen for half-hour sessions once a week for several months. At that time the therapist noted "the most significant defect at the time of evaluation was in right-hand coordination. In speed and accuracy tests, right-hand performance lagged behind the left by approximately one-half. Severe impairment was noted in activities requiring rapidly alternating directional change movements." She was placed on a program stressing the prerequisites for secretarial tasks, electrical stimulation was used and a program of home exercises was instituted. The patient was given speech therapy also in the rehabilitation center.

The final evaluation by the neurologist for disability purposes stated, "Although the patient has sustained neurological disability, she should be able to return to gainful employment, limited only by the amount of dexterity which she might be required to perform in her work." Following rehabilitation, the psychologist's report stated, "Test findings suggest that patient is capable of performing well in a career that demands either verbal or mechanical skills. Her fear of failure might be allayed to a large degree by placing her in business school where she would have a chance to test herself out and gain some confidence."

The patient missed her first appointment with the examiner, and when telephoned indicated that she thought the appointment was for 9:30 P.M., rather than 9:30 A.M. When the examiner expressed surprise that she would think the appointment to be this late in the day, the patient responded that she did not think that would be unusual.

When she appeared for her next appointment, the patient was found to be an attractive, blond-haired lady, well dressed in a pantsuit. She stated that her last employment had been four years previously, when she had been employed as a secretary, an occupation she had pursued for many years. She had gone through tenth grade in high school, then later got her G.E.D. She also went to a business college and had a comptometer course as well.

When asked to describe the results of her accident, the patient stated, "My voice box was hurt, I see double so I guess my eyes were hurt, and the fingers on my right hand were affected." She also indicated that her pelvis had been broken.

When she was questioned closely about how her "voice box was hurt," it soon became apparent that she was talking about aphasia. There was no physical damage to her larynx. She tried to illustrate what she meant by this by saying, "When I was in the hospital, if the nurse came in and said to me, 'Good morning, Betty (pseudonym),' I would say back to her 'Good morning, Betty.' I would only repeat what other people said. That's what I mean about having to learn to talk all over again. I couldn't make my voice box work right."

When asked about her eyes, she stated, "I always thought there was an operation that I could have that would fix my eyes. But I went to the doctor and he said there was nothing he could do for my eyes. And I had to accept that—and about my whole being. That is, that I am normal. I might not seem normal, but I mean I am normal for me. I can't explain it. I mean I can't be any different than I am."

When asked about her hand, she stated, "I can't make the fingers work individually on my right hand well enough to type. My left hand is better off. I practice typing nearly every day. I can only type ten to twenty words per minute."

I asked the patient specifically if her head was injured. She answered, "I really don't know. My mom said my brain was so swollen it almost burst my scalp. I was paralyzed and I know I had to use a walker, but I didn't notice anything about my head. Apparently I had some ribs broken."

We see here the patient's difficulty in accepting the fact of her brain damage. She wished to attribute her visual difficulties, as well as her paralysis, her incoordination, and her speech problems to injury to specific limbs or organs. As is often true in the brain damaged, we see her massive denial of anything "wrong" with her head, or in her particular case, her denial of the fact that she was even injured in her head. Because of her defense against catastrophic anxiety around awareness of brain damage, the patient has presented a picture to examiners of being much more competent and capable than she really is.

The patient was then asked questions designed to evaluate her capacity for employment. When asked, "What were you able to do before the accident that you are no longer able to do?", the patient replied, "I didn't have to practice my typing then. It just came to me easier. I have tried to work as a waitress, but I can't stand the strain of being on my feet that long." When asked exactly what she meant, she stated, "I see double to either side of where I am looking. This disturbs my sense of balance. I have to catch myself when I walk, if I move my eyes, because I feel I am going to fall down. So as it is, I move very slowly, making sure to look exactly straight ahead. If I change my line of sight, it takes several seconds to readjust to the change. Just walking around, I get a feeling of dizziness, it's hard to explain." Here again we see the patient's defensiveness in trying to hide her diplopia by saying, "I can't stand the strain of being on my feet."

When asked how she spends her day, she stated that she found it impossible to watch television because it irritated her, but she tended to blame it on the quality of the program. As she talked about her daily life, it was apparent that her fifteen-year-old daughter was really taking care of the family. The daughter cleaned the house, got the younger children off to school, did the washing and ironing, etc. Again, the patient denied she was incapable of doing these things, leading one to believe that she was really taking care of things around the house. For example, the washer and drier were in the basement of their home, and the patient was afraid to go up and down stairs for fear she might fall, so the daughter did the laundry. She was afraid to go downstairs bcause she had to hold her head straight ahead and could not look down and refocus her eyes for each step. She also stated that she could not vacuum the carpet because it made her dizzy. As it ended up, she was capable only of making the children's beds and going to a grocery store nearby to which she could walk to buy groceries to prepare simple meals.

The more one talked to the patient, the more one was impressed by the disorganization in her thinking. For example, in describing the accident she stated, "We were coming back on the highway and the accident supposedly happened at a certain crossroad. I do not remember anything about it, or two hours before it happened. I was not driving, I was sitting in the driver's seat." We see the incongruity in this last sentence, which was apparent frequently in the paient's speech. Regarding the accident, she said further, "If I remembered the accident, I think it would be terrible for me, but I don't. I don't even want to know where it happened. I put it in the back of my mind and I pretend that it didn't happen."

Mental status examination indicated interference with attention and concentration, and particularly with shifting attention. Surprisingly, abstracting ability seemed intact. Simple calculations were handled adequately, and exploration of her mood indicated denial of depression. For example, when asked if she gets "down in the dumps" about things, she replied brightly, "Oh no, I have never felt sorry for myself. Sometimes I get tears in my eyes when I think about working, but it doesn't get to me."

Bender-Gestalt reproductions indicated a marked visual-perceptual disorder. Some designs were rotated 90 degrees.

Rorschach results indicated a striking difficulty in integration and a tendency to focus on minor details while overlooking more important wholes. Other times, she made customary or popular responses to the cards. However, when questioned as to what it was about the card that reminded her of these things, she pointed to irrelevant or bizarre details to confirm her impressions.

Of special interest regarding the Rorschach performance was

what appeared to be a type of aphasia. She had special difficulties with nouns. For example, to Card V she said 'It looks like one of those—oh, what do you call them—they go like this (made waving motions with arms)." (Examiner. Butterfly?) "Yes, that's it—butterfly." On another card she could not think of the word "hide," saying, "It looks like the outside part, you know, the—outside of an animal."

DIAGNOSTIC IMPRESSION: Chronic brain syndrome, traumatic in origin.

COMMENTS: Employment will be quite difficult for this lady, both because of her visual and motor problems as well as her difficulties in certain types of thinking. It is unclear just what kind of employment she could undertake at this time. Possibly a battery of vocational tests would clarify that question. Employment opportunities will be quite limited for her because of the necessity for her to move slowly to compensate for her visual problem, her partial residual paralysis in her right hand, and her handicap in verbal expression.

She should be considered disabled until such time as vocational training and job placement are accomplished. I believe she is capable of managing her own funds.

A CASE OF ACUTE BRAIN SYNDROME WITH SECONDARY PSYCHOSIS, DUE TO NEOPLASTIC GROWTH

The following case illustrates the usefulness of psychological testing in making a differential diagnosis on a disabled patient. It also illustrates how interview and mental status material can aid in differential diagnoisis.

The patient, a fifty-year-old white male, was referred by the medical doctor of his company to a psychiatrist for evaluation. He was hospitalized by the psychiatrist, and after a period of several days, referred to this examiner for help in "making a differential diagnosis between acute schizophrenia and some kind of brain syndrome."

The patient was found on the ward at the hospital dressed in housecoat and pajamas. He walked very slowly to the testing room. In the initial interview, lapses in attention and concentration were observed, as well as circumstantial thinking and loose associations. It was difficult for him to give an accurate and coherent history, and he seemed easily distracted by extraneous thoughts. He also seemed quite depressed, and at times his voice would break as though he were going to sob.

He described the onset of his problems three weeks previously when he was traveling for his company to a neighboring state. The patient is a foreman for a large construction company. While in the neighboring state, he became forgetful, emotional, and anxious. He also became quite irritable with his men. He described that he would start to say something to one of his employees and was unable to finish the sentence because he could not remember what he wanted to say. He also stated, "I got very emotional like I am now."

After three or four days, the patient flew back to company headquarters to see the company physician. The physician examined him and could find nothing organically wrong, and referred him to the psychiatrist.

In interviewing the patient, his attention seemed to wander and often when asked a question, he replied with an answer that seemed completely irrelevant. For example, when asked his first name, he replied, 'Well, I have two of them; one is Bushy Sam, and the other is Star Bar Joe." The examiner asked if these were the names of his horses, and the patient agreed.

The patient was born and raised on the East Coast, his parents are both living and healthy, he had no siblings, and he was married with two children. He had one year of high school and performed successfully in school, but quit in order to "run away from home" and go to the Southwest where he lived with an aunt and uncle during his teenage years. During that time he did construction work with his uncle and became interested in construction as an occupation.

He worked successfully with various construction companies, and worked his way up to foreman where he had been for the past ten years. He stated that he was well paid on this job. He has never been fired from a job, in spite of the fact that he used to do some heavy drinking in his younger years.

Three times while working in construction jobs he was knocked unconscious in accidents. He was in the Army during WW II, and when asked if he had been in combat he stated, "I was always subject to it." He denied ever having suffered concussion or injury while in the service. No other relevant medical history was elicited.

In exploring the situation at the time he became ill in the neighboring state, the patient was supervising a construction job there, similar to many he had overseen before. He was in charge of the operation, which was not unusual for him. He had not been drinking prior to the day he began to feel ill. No special circumstances could be elicited about that day that were any different from many other days. There were no particular technical problems that could not be handled. The patient recalled waking up in the morning irritable, ate very little breakfast, which was unusual for him, and went directly to the construction site. He recalled feeling "confused," and his men had to repeat questions to him. His memory of those days was somewhat clouded, but foremost in his mind was a feeling of extreme irritability.

MENTAL STATUS TESTING: The patient knew the name of the President of the United States but could not recall the name of the previous president. He could not remember the examiner's name. He knew the city in which he was hospitalized, but could not recall the name of the hospital.

He remembered the place of his birth, his wife's maiden name, and the years of birth of his two children.

The patient was able to recite the alphabet and to count backwards from 20 by 1's, although slowly. He did make one error but corrected himself. He found it impossible to do serial 7 subtractions from 100. He got the first subtraction, 93, but was unable to go any further. He became quite upset at this, repeating over and over, "What is the matter with me?"

It became apparent that the patient was very anxious and also was very embarrassed by his inadequacies. He felt threatened because he could not answer questions. The examiner decided to delete the remainder of the customary mental status examination at this point, and to proceed to psychological testing with selected tests that might provoke less feelings of inadequacy in the patient.

To summarize the interview and mental status material up to this point, we see problems in recent memory, concentration, loose associations, and circumstantial thinking. Thought did not progress in an orderly fashion in the patient, and he seemed very distracted by extraneous or intrusive thoughts. His mood was depressed.

As regards the differential diagnosis, while the symptoms listed above are not inconsistent with the possibility of schizophrenia, we see several important differences. First, in the history we see a very sudden onset of illness in a man fifty years of age who had lived a previously well-adapted and successful vocational life. Furthermore, as far as we knew, his family and social life were also characterized by few problems. He had never been discharged from a job, and he had worked his way up to a management position where he had been financially quite successful.

Secondly, we could find no circumstances on the job the day he became ill that seemed unusual or that required exceptional effort. There was no rational "reason" for the patient to have been under undue stress.

Thirdly, in looking at the quality of the patient's loose associations and his flow of ideas, we see none of the morbid or bizarre quality that we expect to find in schizophrenia. This morbid quality is difficult to describe, but has often been characterized as "blood and guts." It is very different from the example given when the patient named his two horses.

PSYCHOLOGICAL TESTING: Results of the Bender-Gestalt Test showed a visual-perceptual disorder. This was characterized by perseveration, some distortion, and a regression to a perceptual age associated with children of six or eight years.

Results of the Trails Test were markedly within the organic range. Extended time periods to completion as well as errors both confirmed an impression of organic brain damage.

Rorschach test results were commensurate with a severe brain syndrome. Impotency of response, perseveration in the extreme, perplexity and confusion, were all characteristic of his responses. He also exhibited considerable irritability which seemed to spring from his marginal awareness of his totally inadequate performance. Of the ten cards, he rejected two because he was unable to see anything. On the eight remaining cards, seven of them were seen as a "harbor" or "bay." His reality testing was very poor, and his thinking quite concrete. On one card he referred to an area colored red as "mountains" simply because "mountains are off-color." This response was given with complete disregard of the formal blot properties, for the area indicated had no resemblance to mountains. In the only response he gave that was not a harbor or bay, he responded with "some sort of a rat, or a rat hide," and then went on to point out to the examiner the rat's head, body, and *wings.*

DIAGNOSTIC IMPRESSION: Acute brain syndrome, severe, with secondary psychosis, etiology unknown.

COMMENTS: This patient must be considered psychotic because of the degree to which cognitive and intellectual functioning has given way to his organic condition. Neurological consultation is recommended.

With regard to the question of disability, the patient appears totally disabled. He is mentally incompetent as well, and cannot be expected to manage his own funds if he is given a disability allowance.

ADDENDUM: Two weeks following this examination, the referring psychiatrist telephoned the examiner to say that the patient had died in his sleep the previous night. Postmortem examination revealed a large malignant intercranial neoplasm of a fast-growing variety.

A CASE OF CHRONIC MENTAL DETERIORATION SECONDARY TO ALCOHOLISM

This case illustrates a relatively common type of disability patient referred through social agencies, Social Security, or seen at the Veterans Administration. As is typical of these patients, alcoholism or mental deterioration is not claimed by the patient as the basis for disability. Customarily, symptoms are referrable to the limbs or organs, lower back syndrome is common, and less commonly to personality conflicts on the job.

As a general rule, active alcoholics tend to hide or greatly diminish the amount and frequency of alcohol consumption. Often a direct question, such as "Do you drink very much?" is met with an evasive answer, e.g. "not very much" or "just now and then." Sometimes a more direct or even confronting question is more productive, e.g. "How much do you drink?" or even, "Do you drink a pint a day, a quart a day?"

Certain clues to the possibility of chronic alcoholism with mental deterioration can be found in the social history. Typically, the patient has moved around a great deal in terms of employment. Possibly he has migrated around the country to a considerable extent. Certain occupations are associated with disabling alcoholism such as short-order cook, house painter, and day laborer. There is often a history of repeated marriages.

Certain behavior in the doctor's office is not uncommon in this group of patients. Slurred or indistinct speech is often noted, and irratibility is common in response to questions.

In cases where mental deterioration has occurred, a pattern of behavior is typical when the examiner is taking a history. Superficially, it may seem that the patient is answering questions. However, one soon begins to feel frustrated in trying to get hard facts about the employment record or social relationships. There is a certain evasiveness and obliqueness in the patient's replies, often glossed over by an air of confidence in the voice or bravado in recounting accomplishments.

When deficiency in memory is paramount, we see a phenomena of "filling in" information about a past that very possibly never occurred. This phenomena is most apparent is Korsakov's syndrome. At first we may be astounded by what appears to be a remarkable memory on the part of the patient. He will give dates, names, and times of day from twenty or thirty years ago regarding relatively inconsequential happenings.

In the employment history, the reasons for moving from job to job are inevitably glossed over. The patient never states that he was "fired because he was drunk." Often he tends to make previous employments look better than they were.

Medically, a history of brain concussions ("knocked out") is not uncommon. These occur as a result of barroom brawls or being attacked on the streets and robbed. Chronic organic diseases often accompany alcoholism due to malnutrition, excessive alcohol intake, and neglect. These include emphysema, chronic bronchitis, cirrhosis of the liver, venereal diseases, ulcers, and sometimes tuberculosis.

The following case is presented to illustrate some of the difficulties inherent in accurately diagnosing this kind of patient. Although the patient was seen by a variety of physicians for various physical problems, apparently none of them suspected mental deterioration as a possible diagnosis. The reason for this probably lies in the patient's firm, convincing way of speaking and his obliqueness in answering questions.

The patient, a fifty-year-old white male, has managed to make a "pest" of himself in badgering his physicians to judge him to be disabled. He is indeed disabled, but not for the reasons that he presents. His irritability and impatience with his doctors has fostered responses in kind. One physician's report began "This 50-year-old white, obnoxious male was seen in orthopedic clinic . . ."!

The major problem in evaluating this type of patient is one of working with the patient's defensiveness and resistance in order to obtain the information needed to make an accurate diagnosis. The inexperienced examiner may be "put off" by the patient's defensiveness and irritability and want to terminate the interview prematurely.

Some aspects of interviewing this type of patient are presented here. Details of the mental status exam and the psychological testing are not elaborated.

CLINICAL INTERVIEW: Accompanying information with the referral indicated that the patient had had two surgical procedures in the past year for release of flexion contractures in the right and left hands. The procedures were judged successful and the patient participated in physiotherapy for several months to the point where he achieved near-normal use of both hands. He was judged competent and able to return to work. Also noted in the medical information is reference to possible emphysema and questionable active tuberculosis.

In spite of being judged competent by his physicians, the patient had returned several times claiming disability although physiological tests and clinical examination did not reveal more than slight loss of function of the hands. Nevertheless, the patient insisted that he was disabled and consequently was sent to a psychiatrist who diagnosed a "conversion reaction" in relation to the hands. Group therapy was recommended for the patient but he declined. He persisted in his claims of disability and finally was sent to a mental examiner by his agency for evaluation of disability.

The patient stated that his work history had been largely in the State of Colorado except that he "spent winters" in California. In taking a work history, it was difficult for the examiner to pin down exactly the type of work the patient had been doing and when it occurred. When asked what kind of work he had done, he stated that he had primarily done farming. The following exchange then took place:

Examiner: What sort of farming did you do?

Patient: I leveled land in California for irrigation.
You use a Caterpillar tractor and a leveler, and you grade it so that the water will drain.

Examiner: Do you mean you were employed as a heavy machinery operator?

Patient: I've done row cropping such as cotton, corn, lettuce, cultivation, and irrigation.

Examiner: I gather you worked as a hired hand then?

Patient: Well, in Colorado I did ranching. I worked with cattle, calves, did vaccinating, castrating, that sort of thing.

Examiner: You were a hired hand, then?

Patient: Well, it depends. If you've got your cattle, you do them. If you're the most qualified, the other men work under you. If they are more qualified, you work under them. I raised dates in California for several years.

Examiner: Tell me more about that.

Patient: I've done a lot of different things. I drove a truck in California for awhile, too.

On another occasion, the patient mentioned working in Texas. When asked what he was doing in Texas, the patient replied irritably, "I was a dock worker. I told you that before. You probably look down on dock workers."

Up to this point, we see by the patient's evasiveness that he felt embarrassed by what probably was a history of a migrant worker and day laborer in the past few years. This degree of defensiveness tells us that it would probably not be productive, and would, in fact, probably jeopardize the alliance between examiner and patient, to ask him a question directly about why he has moved around so much, or the reasons for termination of these various employments. Instead, it seems best to encourage the patient to continue talking and hope that more information will emerge as times goes on.

At one point the patient mentioned that he was planning to "join IBM" when he working in a large city in the South. When asked to tell more about that, the patient replied as follows:

"Well, it's when I went to the Veterans Administration Hospital there. I wanted them to operate on my hands so I could open them up. I was always getting hurt because I would drop things. They put me on the operating table. I remember it very well. I was on the operating table, and the doctors were all around me, and they were ready to give me a shot to knock me out. Then they decided that I wasn't eligible for VA treatment. Them damned doctors lied to me. That happened twice, that they had me on the operating table ready to go. The last time was August 14, 1969. Then they sent me this social worker who said she was going to send me to school, and she had me all lined up to go to IBM. She was going to send me to a little junior college there to learn how to go to IBM, but then them damn doctors lied and screwed the whole thing up."

In the above paragraph, we see the confusion in the patient's though processes, the looseness of associations, and a suspicious and possibly paranoid attitude about being taken advantage of by others.

In taking a school history, when asked how far he had gone to school, the patient said "I went fourteen years."

Examiner: You didn't finish high school then?

Patient: Well, I was taking this GED exam in California after the service.

Examiner: You got your degree then?

Patient: I told you I completed 14 years. But I didn't actually go to the third or the seventh grades.

Examiner: Why was that?

Patient: I had exceptionally good teachers, so I skipped two grades. In the fourth grade I could do high school math. The teacher gave me trigonometry problems in the fourth grade.

Examiner: You must be pretty good at math. Did you finally get your degree then?

Patient: I went into the service at seventeen. They made me a medic but I rebelled the whole time I was there.

Examiner: What do you mean?

Patient: I did diet work, and worked the VD clinic, but in the first place I can't work with women. I won't take orders from women.

In the above interchange, we see the patient's evasiveness in answering direct questions, his changing the subject, and his defensiveness in owning up to something that he imagined might put him in a "bad light" such as the probability that he did not graduate from high school.

When asked later about drinking, the patient replied, "I used to drink heavy years ago and then I quit. Now I only drink beer. Just about a six-pack a day."

The patient told of living alone in a sleeping room, which has been his style the last few years. He had been married "more than once," but he felt that women cannot be trusted. When asked how he spent his time, he stated that he would go down and "see the boys" at the neighborhood bar now and then, but that he is always home in the evenings because he could not trust people on the streets. He admitted that he had been "beaten up" twice, and when pressed admitted that these beatings occurred "associated with barrooms."

MENTAL STATUS EXAM: Mental status examination as well as psychological testing all confirmed the impression of a chronic brain syndrome. Difficulties in attention, concentration, memory, abstract thought, and ability to do calculations were all present.

Also apparent was a suspicious, somewhat paranoid attitude about people.

COMMENTS: At the end of the examination, after having spent about two and one-half hours with the patient, when informed that he was finished, the patient asked, "Why do they send me to a headshrinker when my problem is with my hands? I don't get it. I've been trying to tell them I'm disabled but they don't think I am. What do you think, Doc?"

This provided an opportunity, coming from the patient himself, for the examiner to share his impressions with the patient and also the possibility to be of some help to him. It also incidentally afforded an opportunity to get considerably more information from the patient. The examiner responded honestly by saying to the patient, "I think your drinking hasn't done your brain much good."

With this stimulus, and thinking that the exam was over and he could talk "freely," the patient related the following:

"That's what my sister tells me. She says I've screwed up my brains. But I don't drink anything like I used to, when I was on the hard stuff. That was when I was cooking in Seattle."

"Did you drink a quart a day?"

"Oh, yes, at least, for years. But then it scared me. I would start having spells of several hours or a day or more that I couldn't remember. I would wake up in the alley, or someplace where I had never been. So since then I don't drink any hard stuff. Now I just drink beer. About a case a day. But I don't even drink that steady anymore.

"Well, sometimes I might get on a good drunk for a month, but then I'll go two or three weeks without a drink. I can't drink like I used to because of my lungs. But like this morning, I woke up at five o'clock and I had five beers there so I just drank them. It seemed to be the thing to do. But I feel good today, because I've been sober since Saturday.

"I can't think as fast as I used to. I used to be able to do five-digit multiplications in my head. Now I do good to do one. Sometimes I can't remember how to spell a word that I have spelled all my life. I tried to write my sister a note the other day, but my spelling was so bad I don't think she could have read it, so I threw it away. But I'm gonna be all right, I think. Since I got off the hard stuff, I think it'll be all right."

This information clarifies for us the probable etiology of the patient's mental deterioration. He has consumed over a quart of whiskey a day for many years, and still drinks a case of beer a day.

This also clarified the rather puzzling fashion in which the patient responded to questions. What seemed to be defensiveness and evasiveness could now be understood as a compensation for memory loss. The patient avoided answering direct questions with factual information because in reality he simply could not remember. Consequently, he avoided the question, or he filled in information and details that lacked a factual basis.

DIAGNOSTIC IMPRESSION: (1) Chronic mental deterioration, secondary to alcoholism; (2) possible Korsakov's syndrome.

COMMENTS: This patient is most certainly disabled on a mental basis. He possibly could do some kinds of day labor between spells of drunkenness, but cannot be expected to be significantly gainfully employed. The treatment of choice is referral to a rehabilitation center for alcoholism, although the examiner is not very optimistic about the patient's accepting this recommendation.

It is impossible to know what sort of employee he might have been prior to his mental deterioration. That information is not available to us from the patient, but could possibly be determined by interviews with relatives or friends of the patient. He cannot be expected to manage his own funds.

A CASE OF CHRONIC SCHIZOPHRENIA

The following illustrates a rather typical case of chronic schizophrenia. It points out the necessity of trying to make an effort to rehabilitate this type of disability patient if at all possible, to prevent secondary gains arising from the disability allowance. Simply diagnosing the patient's condition is not an adequate disability examination. As in this case, recommendations were made to the social agency and to the patient herself.

CLINICAL INTERVIEW: The patient was a twenty-two-year-old

white female found to be an obese girl, with an unkempt look. She wore tennis shoes, no hose, her hair was long and uncombed, and she wore a shapeless homemade dress. Sitting in the waiting room, she seemed to be mumbling or talking to herself. As she came into the office, she was talking to herself in an audible fashion.

When interviewed about her family background, the patient recounted a rather tragic story of a very chaotic home life involving divorced parents and a rejecting stepfather. Eventually the patient's mother divorced her stepfather, and in later adolescence she made attempts to live with her real father as well as her stepfather on several occasions, but neither of them wanted her. Altercations with her mother during adolescence led to her being sent to a private school.

After she talked of these painful memories of early childhood, the examiner reflected sympathetically that she had had a "rough time." At that point she immediately slipped into a psychotic defense. She stated, "At high school they gave me a scientific course because I am a scientific genius. I've been rated as such. I don't know why scientists don't use my ideas, they would save a lot of lives, especially the President. One idea I have would be a force shield—a hardening of the gravity in the air that would protect you from anything including a laser blast. It would be run by a solar battery and would have to be transistorized and put on a belt so you could turn it off and on. That way, no one could possibly hurt you. Another idea would be that the scientists would test and gather together all the people who are telepathic, and send them to the Communist countries, where they could pretend to be tourists. They could read the minds of the Communist leaders. I don't understand why they can't use that idea."

When asked about past employment, the patient said she had done greenhouse work, power sewing, and telephone solicitation for two different agencies. She ordinarily lost her job "for no reason at all." She was discharged from one job because her employer said she was emotionally unstable, "but I didn't like him either." In doing telephone solicitation, she was told she was not producing enough results. She stated, "I can't stand pressure. Any time I have the least pressure, I break—I can't take it. If I am calling people for volunteer work, for example, and they turn me down, I slam down the phone and get angry. Or I'll call them back up again and get really nasty."

When asked what kind of work she would really like to do, she stated very quickly, "I would like to be singing in nightclubs around town. I want to do folk singing professionally." The patient had had no training in singing and no experiece, which demostrates how unrealistic she was in her expectations for herself. Another example of how self-defeating and unrealistic she was, can be seen by her statement that she knits baby blankets to sell. When asked about the price of them, she went on to say that they cost her $8 each for the yarn, and she charges $2 when she sells them. When it was pointed out to her that she loses money, she stated "I know it, but I sell to the poor people because I know what it is like to be poor." It takes her about one month to knit a baby blanket.

When asked about previous psychiatric care, the patient stated that during adolescence she went to a psychiatric clinic as an outpatient for three months, but "the doctor said there wasn't anything wrong with me emotionally." More recently she had been to a community mental health center. "They didn't do anything for me. They gave me some medication that made me dizzy."

When asked about her medical history, the patient was aware only of her obesity as a medical problem. Questions related to neurological functioning were all answered negatively.

The patient's school history indicated that she was an average student, but she quit high school at the end of her junior year "because I was bored." Further exploration indicated that she became acutely self-conscious because of her weight and her social isolation, and preferred to leave school and live alone in a small apartment. She believed that she was educating herself by going to the library frequently where she read books concerning spiritual matters and occult sciences.

When asked how she spent her time, in addition to going to the library, the patient watched TV in her one-room apartment, and walked to a neighboring grocery store where she bought her own food, much of it starches and sweets. She was living on welfare payments.

MENTAL STATUS EXAM: Patient was oriented as to time, place and person. She was able to recite the alphabet and to count backwards from 20 by 1's. She refused to attempt serial 7 subtractions from 100, saying "I was never very good at that."

Responses to proverbs were not concrete, but were inclined to be bizarre and highly personalized. For example, to "When the cat's away, the mice will play," she replied, "When God looks the other way, somebody might try to get away with something, but I don't because I know God's watching me." Responses to similarities were adequately abstract.

When asked about visual and auditory hallucinations, the patient stated, "I don't want to talk about things like that."

The patient denied any problems with memory, recent or remote. She described being "forgetful" about eating the right kind of food and buying sweets instead. When given the name of three objects in the room to recall, she recalled correctly all three after a five-minute interval.

The patient revealed disordered thought processes. When asked questions that demanded factual answers, she often replied with her associations to the question. Generally, these were questions which called for answers that confronted the patient with feelings of loss of self-esteem and inadequacy. Her fanciful responses could be seen as a defense against painful feelings of loss of self-esteem. This was particularly apparent when she was asked to do arithmetic calculations that she found difficult. A typical reply when asked to do a calculation was, "My stepfather said I was a moron, but he didn't realize I was really a genius."

When asked about her mood, the patient stated that she thought she was usually "happy." She denied difficulties in sleeping, but sleeps very irregular hours. Sometimes she stays up all night and will sleep all the next day. Her appetite is obviously good and she denied any problems with constipation.

PSYCHOLOGICAL TESTING: The Rorschach test was administered and the results indicated a chronic psychotic disorder, schizophrenic type. The record is not that of an acute disorder, but rather that of a stabilized chronic condition. She showed the typical "contamination" of responses of schizophrenics, such as her response to Card IV, "a cross between a frog and a fish," and regressive responses such as "a set of twins in a womb." Autistic thinking was elicited by some of the cards, usually dealing with mystical forces or electronic emanations. The record was not chaotic in its entirety, and reality testing broke down only under stress. She was capable of perceiving many of the cards in a conventional fashion. This latter aspect is what gives the record its chronic rather than an acute quality.

DIAGNOSTIC IMPRESSION: Chronic schizophrenia.

COMMENTS: The examiner viewed this patient at that time as severely disabled. She seemed unable to cope with almost any pressure on a job that activates her profound feelings of inferiority and inadequacy, to which she reacts with outburst of anger. However, with some rather extensive kind of corrective experience, she might be more self-sustaining in time.

If disability is allowed, some kind of treatment should be required of the patient. A psychiatric day care program to help her learn some routines of daily living, as well as to provide her with a more adequate diet at least at the noon meal is suggested. It is further recommended that a boarding home placement be considered for her rather than her present one-room apartment where she lives alone. This would increase her contact with other people, aid in socialization, and also guarantee her more regular kinds of meals.

It is the impression of the examiner that with a year or two of a regime of habit training and a more regulated life, it is possible she could become at least partially self-sustaining in a job situation. At twenty-two years of age, this patient should not be considered "hopeless" until a vigorous effort has been made at rehabilitation.

These possible arrangements were discussed with the patient and she seemed little interested. However, it is obvious that she was not going to change her lifestyle without some sort of intervention as well as a "lever" to get her moving.

In sum, the patient can be considered currently disabled but possibly rehabilitatable. It is doubtful that this patient is capable of managing her funds in her best interests. One conceives the possibility of her giving her money away to "poor people." For her own protection a guardian for her funds should be appointed.

A CASE OF POSTTRAUMATIC NEUROSIS

The traumatic neurosis is related to an anxiety neurosis, but precipitated by external environmental factors in most cases, such as war experiences or accidents. The fact that one person develops a traumatic neurosis under these circumstances, whereas another does not, suggests the existence of historical antecedents that predispose the patient to become ill.

It is possible, with psychotherapy, to assist the patient in understanding the relationship between the traumatic event in the present and its relevance to the past. "In-depth" understanding may not always be necessary, and some workers have found that a "re-living" of the traumatic event may be enough for symptomatic improvement. This technique was employed in World War II and following with good results. (26).

In the following case, a traumatic event brought about psychiatric symptom formation in the patient that was not apparent prior to the accident. He became aware of internal turmoil, but connected it to the accident only in a physical sense. His suit for financial compensation was on a physical basis, but not substantiated by physical examination.

As is sometimes the case, the physician declared the patient competent and not disabled, without taking into account the psychological effects of the traumatic event. Of course, the patient himself did not connect his subjective impression of disability to the traumatic event either, so he could not explain to his doctor how he felt disabled except to focus on organic structure.

It is helpful for us to remember that when a patient claims he is disabled, he is talking about *something*. In only rare cases is he simply lying or malingering. If the physician cannot find organic disability, he might ask himself, "Is there any other way in which this patient can feel disabled, even though he cannot explain it to me?" Exploration of this question may lead to an evaluation for mental disability.

This attitude can help prevent the sort of humiliation that occurs too often, when the physician tells the patient, "There is nothing wrong with you," and the patient *knows* at some inarticulate level that there *is* something "wrong" with him.

In the following case, the patient was referred by a neurologist with the concurrence of the patient's attorney. The patient was a thirty-four-year-old white male. He was suing a major industry, claiming disability as the result of a motor vehicle accident, and requesting financial compensation. The patient claimed brain damage as well as back injury. The neurologist examined the patient and could find no evidence of neurological disorder or disease.

This case illustrates the importance of school and employment history, as well as the concept of "before and after" contrasts.

The patient was born and raised on the West Coast. He has two siblings, both older. His parents are deceased of natural causes, his father of a "stroke" and his mother of pneumonia.

He went to public school, finishing sixth grade, and then withdrew from school. When asked why he quit school, he replied, "After my father died I had to go to work and help my mother." He stated he was fourteen years of age when he quit, so we might assume that he was held back one or two grades, although he denies this. He stated that he did "pretty well" in school although he always had some difficulty with arithmetic.

His work began in a grocery store, stocking produce. He worked there for several years, but after his mother died, he moved to a different town and worked in an amusement park running the merry-go-round. He voluntarily terminated that job and in 1969 moved to Denver where he was first employed in a restaurant as a cook. After about two years, he terminated that job and began his most recent employment, working in a small factory that makes steel bands and clamps.

The patient worked at his most recent employment for about four years prior to his accident. It was necessary for us to give considerable attention to the nature of the work he did with his company in order to furnish us with some kind of baseline on which to judge possible deterioration of functioning and disability.

With this firm he worked at four different jobs. The first job was working on a drill press where he "drilled holes in little blocks of steel." He performed that work satisfactorily, and was transferred to another job which interested him more, involving working at a mill. He stated that this job required more skill. He described it as milling tools and reaming them.

The examiner questioned him at some length regarding his exact duties. It was necessary for him to set certain gauges on a machine. Although the machine was largely automatic, the patient had to make adjustments for different products. In these adjustments, he occasionally used a micrometer, a ruler, and did some minor arithmetic subtraction at times but ordinarily he used printed tables furnished him by the employer.

After working with this machine, he was transferred to a machine that involved band winding. When asked why he was transferred, he stated that he volunteered to be transferred because the band-winding machine position paid more money because it was more hazardous. This involved running a machine that would wind bands into a roll. It was necessary for him to shut off the machine and cut the band when the roll was filled, and then to refeed the machine with a new band in order to start a new roll. It was while working at this band-winding machine that he suffered the accident that will be described below.

It was important at this point for us to note that *following* his accident he *returned* to his place of employment, and was transferred to a machine that made clamps. The reason for his transfer was that the band-winding machine position had been filled in his absence. He made clamps for securing boxcar air hoses, for installing signs on posts, etc. In this job, it was necessary for him to feed wire or other material into a machine which manufactured the clamps. It was necessary for him to set the machine by certain gauges for various sizes of clamps. Again, the machine was largely automatic, and as the material was produced, it was his duty to box the material and label the boxes.

He did this work satisfactorily, but after a period of about three weeks the patient quit working voluntarily because he stated that his back and neck hurt him. He felt that the pain he was experiencing in his back and neck were a result of his accident. When asked if he felt he could return to this last job and do that kind of work again, he stated that he could do band-winding and clamps immediately if his back did not bother him, but that it was painful for him to stand or sit in one position. He volunteered spontaneously that he probably could return to the milling job after becoming reacquainted with that machine. We note here that the patient's reason for feeling that he is disabled and unable to return to his job involves his discomfort with his back and neck.

The examiner questioned the patient at this point as to whether he felt there were any other reasons that he could not return to his old job and do the work, and he stated that he could not think of any. When asked directly if he felt that he could not do the work for any "mental" reason, he paused to consider the question and then answered "no."

He then amended that answer, rather hastily, by saying that he could not memorize things anymore, and specifically stated, "If my wife sent me to the store to buy two or three items, I would not be able to remember them; I would have to write them down." We note that the reference to going to the store is a standard question often asked by examiners to test memory functions. He went on to say that he had trouble remembering his phone number, certain dates such as the anniversary of his marriage, and the birthdays of his children. He believed that he "used to" remember those dates without any difficulty. He also referred at this point to what he described as amnesia which followed the accident.

The patient described his accident as follows. In the summer of the previous year he was struck on the driver's side of his car by a truck owned or contracted for by a large industry. The driver of the truck allegedly pleaded guilty and was ticketed for the accident. As the patient described the accident, he was somewhat circumstantial in his thinking. That is, when asked simply to tell what happened, he went into great detail about events immediately prior to the accident. For example, he said he went to a department store in the shopping center to buy a new jacket, that he could not find one his correct size, that he tried another store, etc. It took him several minutes of this sort of preliminary description before he came to the actual accident itself. This circumstantiality in thinking is diagnostically most often found in organic disorders and/or anxiety states. He went on to say he was hit by the truck which he did not see, following which he suffered a lapse of memory.

This lapse of memory was the "amnesia" that the patient spoke about. However, it was not always a complete amnesia because he recalled a series of events that occurred during the next few days, and his memory seemed to wax and wane in this regard. For example, he had memories of hearing sirens, being placed in an ambulance, having his back Xrayed, being discharged from the hospital once and returning the next day. He also recalled that he had a "back operation," apparently a laminectomy, for an extruded disc. He had vague memories of returning to his home following surgery, and that his wife was upset with him for his irascibility and short temper.

About three months after the accident his memory returned and events from that time onward were intact in his memory. He attributed the return of his memory to talking about the accident with his brother-in-law. It is important to note here that if, as was alleged, the patient's memory returned as a result of his talks with his brother-in-law, it is likely we are not dealing with an organically based amnesia, but with a psychologically based amnesia.

When asked why it is that he feels he is no longer able to work, he stated that he was in constant pain that originated in his back and neck, that he was having trouble with his memory, that he had gone through a period of amnesia, that he could not concentrate, and that he suffered from constant feelings of nervousness and low spirits.

We note here especially the fact that the patient did return to his employment after the accident and worked for a period of about three weeks. He voluntarily terminated that job, which presumes his work was satisfactory. Thus we see that he was not organically unable to do the work, but that he rather suffered from pain. The neurological symptoms he refers to, such as amnesia, memory problems, and problems in concentration, were not pleaded as factors in his terminating his job after he returned.

In obtaining the patient's impression of his medical history, he stated that he was currently taking no medications except aspirin for his back and neck. When asked about previous hospitalizations, the patient stated that about one year *prior* to the accident he was in the hospital for "back trouble" and was treated by heat application and bed rest. The patient was released from the hospital and experienced no further back problems until the accident.

More questions regarding medical history revealed that the patient had suffered from asthma "all my life," and he also mentioned what he considered to be either bronchitis or emphysema. In interview he did have a noticeable "wheeze" to his breathing.

The patient denied ever having been unconscious or suffering blows to the head, except in the case of his recent accident. He did suffer a left-sided headache following the accident. He stated that he does not indulge in alcohol more than social drinking. He denied any "fits or spells," convulsions, or epileptic seizures. He denied hallucinations, visual or auditory, and further denied ever having had either syphillis or gonorrhea.

Exploring sensory phenomena, he admitted to no unusual tastes, smells, visual images, auditory alterations, sensitivity to light or sound, dizziness, numbness, or fainting spells. He described his current "mental" symptoms as irritability, difficulty with memory, getting easily upset, and irritations with his children. He also stated he gets a "funny feeling" which he decribed as a feeling of confusion. He admitted to no problems with balance, awkwardness, cluminess, or incoordination.

Presently, the patient is on welfare. He spends the time around the house with his wife and children. They may sometimes go to the laundry together, or take the children to the park.

Of special note here is the fact that the patient engages considerable time in a hobby which has turned into a source of modest income. He makes pictures with small mosaic tiles, which he glues to a masonite board, and frames and sells to friends and neighbors for about $20 each. He discovered this hobby and designs for the pictures in a hobby magazine. The work is somewhat intricate, requiring considerable coordination and attention to detail. He stated that with concentrated effort he can make a picture, complete, in three hours. This includes gluing the tiles, framing the picture, and stringing the wire on the back for hanging.

The point here on which we wish to focus our attention is that producing these pictures requires certainly a normal attention span and concentration, as well as visual motor coordination. These are mental functions that are particularly vulnerable to brain damage.

MENTAL STATUS EXAM: On mental status examination, the patient was oriented as to person, place, and time. He knew correctly the address of the examiner's office, the day of the week, and his own address.

When asked about memory, he believed that his memory "isn't what it used to be before the accident." He was able to recite the alphabet, recalled the West Coast city in which he lived during his early years, the street on which he lived, and even the house address. He thinks he "might" have trouble remembering the names of some of his old friends, but he was not sure. He correctly identified the name of the President of the United States, and the two presidents prior to him.

When given the names of three objects in the room and asked to recall them five minutes later, he remembered correctly two of the three. He stated that he is able to find his way around the city satisfactorily and he does not get lost. When questioned, he gave some recent current events that had been on television.

The patient was able to count backwards from 20 by 1's, although slowly. He was able to recite the alphabet correctly. When asked to do serial 7 subtractions from 100, he found this task very difficult. He could not get beyond the first two subtractions.

The patient's difficulty with serial 7 subtractions is somewhat puzzling. Pronounced difficulty with this task is often a sign of some possible organic damage. On the other hand, we noted the patient's visible anxiety, his low educational level, and his admission that arithmetic had always been his most difficult subject.

In response to proverbs, the patient's answers varied between abstract and personalized. He did not give concrete answers, which would be typical of organic damage. Responses to similarities were likewise not concrete.

There was no evidence of paranoid thought content. He has always suffered from feelings of inadequacy, however. Throughout his life he was aware of his low educational achievement and felt that it "showed" in talking to other people or employers. He has never been particularly friendly with his neighbors, feeling that he should "keep in his place." It was only on his most recent employment that he began to feel increased feelings of esteem.

At first he was actually surprised that he could run the machines at the factory. For the first time in his life, he began to feel somewhat successful. He now believes that his newfound feeling of success is "all ruined" since his accident, and he tended to feel that his neighbors look down on him as a "goof-off" because he was not working.

The patient admitted to suffering from a chronic mild depression since the time of his accident. Most of the time he sleeps well and his appetite is satisfactory. He has never considered suicide, and when he feels quite depressed he will go to a bar and drink too much, and then go home and sleep it off.

He worries a good deal of the time about not being able to return to work. On the other hand, he has not actually tried working because he feels convinced that he cannot put in a full day's work because of his back pain. Presently, when his back begins to hurt he lies down on the couch or on the bed. He watches TV a good deal of the time and feels quite emotional and cries when he watches programs that deal with hospitals and patients. He stated that these kinds of programs make him "feel bad" and remind him of what has happened to him.

Sometimes he thinks about the accident when his mind is not occupied with other things. He tries to review the events in his mind and tries to remember the truck striking his car. Sometimes he has a picture of it in his mind, of the car rolling over, and he fantasies about what would have happened had he been thrown out. He has a visual image of himself being crushed underneath the car or under the wheels of the truck. Although he cannot remember it directly, he tries to imagine the truck bearing down on his car and what it must have been like at the moment of impact. These thoughts usually come to him when he is resting, and they make him so nervous that he will get up and take a walk to "take his mind off of it."

PSYCHOLOGICAL TESTING: Intelligence test results rather consistently came out at a low average intellectual level. This was true of the performance scale as well, a scale particularly sensitive to brain damage. A pronounced and consistent tremor in the hands was noticed as the patient worked with blocks. This was not an intermittent or intention tremor as is sometimes seen in organic conditions but a consistent tremor that could be explained on the basis of anxiety.

The patient's reproduction of Bender-Gestalt figures indicated good visual perceptual accuracy. A great deal of tension was noted in the line quality, suggestive of anxiety but not necessarily organicity.

Results of the Trails Test were within the normal range.

On the Wide Range Achievement Test, the patient scored seventh grade in reading, and fourth grade in arithmetic. In reading, he frequently mispronounced simple words which, when asked to repeat, he then pronounced correctly. The fact that he was able to correct his errors in reading indicated an important diagnostic consideration. That is to say, we were not dealing with dyslexia, an organically based reading problem, for in the case of dyslexia correction cannot be made without special training and education. Again, anxiety is the most likely cause.

On the Rorschach Test, the patient's responses indicated no psychosis or impending psychotic process. Typical organic indicators such as perseveration, over-attention to detail, difficulty in integration, and color naming, were absent. Rather we saw a somewhat neurotic record involving mild to moderate depression, passivity, dependency, and feelings of lack of masculinity. We also see evidence of mild to moderate anxiety.

DIAGNOSTIC IMPRESSION: Posttraumatic neurosis.

COMMENTS: We did not have sufficient test evidence to justify a diagnosis of organic brain dysfunction. Certain signs, while equivocal, were not definitive. Psychological test evidence as well as interview evidence indicated current anxiety, which appeared to have originated at the time of the accident. We also saw mild to moderate depression. Diagnostically, the patient would best fit a conceptualization of post traumatic neurosis.

Obviously, the accident had a great deal of meaning for the patient psychologically as well as physically. He had begun to feel self-respect and a heightened sense of self-esteem for the first time in his life when he was working at the factory. There is some evidence to suggest that he felt that he did not "deserve" this newfound status and that it weighed rather uneasily on his shoulders. He feels that this was all "taken way" from him at the time of the accident, which probably has deep-seated psychological meaning for him centered around anxiety about success and potency.

Regarding disability, the examiner shared with the neurologist the opinion that this patient did not demonstrate sufficient evidence for a diagnosis of brain syndrome. Nevertheless, he was at this time disabled in that it was his firm conviction that he was not able to work. He was obsessed with repetitive thoughts of the accident, and he suffered from discomforting anxiety and mild depression. He had lost his sense of self-esteem and believed that he was incapable of coping with employment.

I believe that psychotherapy could be of considerable benefit to this man. It would certainly be a mistake to consider him permanently disabled. In exploring this question with him, he stated that he would be willing to see a psychotherapist if it could bring some relief from anxiety. He agreed to apply for help at a local outpatient mental health center. Since it has been less than a year's time since the accident, the prognosis for psychotherapy is reasonably good in this case.

In sum, I would view this patient as temporarily disabled, and recommend a reevaluation after a trial of psychotherapy.

A CASE OF HYPOCHRONDRIASIS

This case was selected to illustrate how hypochondriasis is often a "mixed bag" as far as the diagnostic picture is concerned. Hypochondriasis often overlays a more basic passive-dependent orientation to life. The onset of the illness, as in this case, can begin as a traumatic or war neurosis which, if left untreated, begins to focus itself on bodily functions and organ systems. The phrase, "if left untreated," may also imply by omission an iatrogenic feature. That is to say, if the patient is judged "disabled" on what he assumes to be a physical basis, his hypochondriacal symptomatology is reinforced. Consequently, the diagnosis of "hypochondriasis" as differentiated from some other diagnosis, such as "traumatic neurosis" or "anxiety neurosis," is dependent upon what "level" of interpertation we wish to make of the illness. "Hypochondriasis" is more descriptive, whereas "traumatic neurosis" is more generic.

The patient was a forty-nine-year-old white male who was referred for evaluation by a public agency. He was found to be a neatly dressed man who wore a neck brace. He had driven to the office in his car. As he sat down, he pointed out that he had a "phlebitis leg" which was wrapped in an elastic bandage. He went on to say that this was his fifth or sixth application to the agency for disability insurance, and that he had been turned down on his previous claims. All of the previous claims involved various bodily organs or organ systems.

The patient lived with his mother, age seventy. His parents were separated before the patient was two years of age, and he has never seen his father who is dead. He has no brothers and sisters, and was raised in his mother's home largely by a grandmother and an aunt. He went through eight years of school, and a few years later went into Civilian Conservation Corps camps for about nine months, and from there into the Army in 1940.

He served throughout World War II as an administrative sergeant. While serving in the Army in Belgium, he was subjected to V-2 bombardments for several months. He still has nightmares about this, thirty years later. He recalled witnessing a little boy blown to bits by a bomb. After several months of this, he was diagnosed as having a "nervous problem" and was shipped to the United States to a military hospital near the end of the war where he was given a medical discharge and was judged to have "100% disability," service connected. He has since that time received a monthly pension check from the Veterans Administration.

After his discharge he wanted to reenlist in the Army, hoping to make it a career, but was not allowed to do so. He was not given any psychological treatment at that time. This was most unfortunate, because it has left him a chronic psychological cripple, which was reinforced by secondary gains from his pension ever since.

I questioned him extensively regarding his work history since his discharge from the Army. When asked "What difficulties do you have when you try to work?", he launched into an extensive enumeration of a variety of work experiences, most of which terminated in his resignation or walking off the job, and a few of which were terminated by his employer because of lost working time due to illness. In going through his work history, the patient enumerated in each case the physical symptoms that resulted in leaving the job. A brief summary of these follow.

His first job after discharge was working for a Federal agency as a clerk, which lasted a period of about four months, and the patient then "got sick from nerves." His next job was as a cook at a restaurant which was terminated when the patient "went to pieces because the waiters hollered at me." He next worked as a bartender and lost that job because he would "get rattled." His next job was again a clerical one which he had to terminate because he developed a problem in his handwriting and could no longer write.

There is a progression in the patient's explanations of his terminations from jobs over the years. As noted above, at first his explanations took the form of "nerves" in some fashion. As the years went on, however, they began to take the form of various physical ailments. The patient stated that he had spent many months in the hospital with a pulmonary embolism and arthritis in the cervical area. The arthritis also goes across his shoulders, down his back, and into his left arm. He used to have "beautiful" handwriting, but now he is unable to even sign his name. He states, "I can't even write a note to my mother." (The patient had no difficulty doing the Bender test later, which requires good coordination.) He broke into tears, he stated, whenever he talked to a potential employer, and consequently "Who would hire me?"

He would get "spells" like someone was sitting on his chest

and he would be unable to breathe. He was unable to sleep at night, sometimes continuing for a period of two or three days. His "spells" caused him to "pass out." He went to a doctor who allegedly suggested that he may have had a seizure. Another doctor stated that he did not have epilepsy, but "of course, that was a government doctor and they don't care about you." He had a "nervous stomach" and at times had difficulty hearing. "My ears have been ringing ever since 1944." A doctor told him he might have some nerve deafness.

When mentioning his ears, he thought of his eyes, and mentioned he had gone to the eye doctor and "he said I had a lazy left eye." He used to enjoy reading books, but doesn't any more, because "my mother said I had the Hong Kong flu." He had claustrophobia and could not go into elevators. His blood and urine "have turned to water."

It was rather amazing in talking to this man, to observe the degree to which he clung tenaciously to the position that he was a "lost cause" as far as possible employment is concerned. It began the moment he walked in the room, and ended with his last words at the door as he left. He reviewed his bodily systems one by one, pointing out the various disorders involved in each one, and actually seemed to think of things that he had not thought of before as he was talking. His last words as he rose from his chair and stretched, were "Oh, my back. I don't know when they're going to do something for my back. I'll have to file on it next."

MENTAL STATUS EXAM: Mental status testing did not suggest difficulties with memory, concentration, abstract thought, or ability to do calculations. Throughout the mental status examination the patient professed great feelings of inadequacy and incapability, but when pressed to produce answers, could do so. Investigation of mood indicated a mild chronic depression, and social relationships were disordered in the sense that the patient had few friends and little or no interests and activities. The most important person in his life was his mother, and although he had been married several years, it appeared as through he did not become genuinely emotionally invested in his wife.

PSYCHOLOGICAL TESTING: Psychological testing correlated with the mental status exam in the sense that it revealed no difficulties in the patient's sensorium. Indications of organic brain syndrome were largely negative.

Rorschach results were consistent with a passive aggressive-passive dependent disorder. More importantly, the Rorschach indicated the roots of the patient's anxiety neurosis. Several of his perceptions seemed to be in reference to war experiences. For example, he saw "V-2's just like the Germans had," or "a plane coming out of the clouds," or "You might say that this is England and this is France, with the channel down the middle."

In recent years, the patient had gone to the Veterans Administration Hospital for psychological assistance. He did not begin this program until many years after his discharge from the service, however. In exploring with him the nature of his treatment at the V.A., we note that he accepted little or no responsibility for his feelings. For example, although he has had three years of exposure to group therapy and other kinds of day care programs at the V.A., in explaining why he cries frequently he stated with wonderment and naivete, "the psychologist at the V.A. told me that crying is due to emotion."

DIAGNOSTIC IMPRESSION: Hypochondrical disorder, severe.

COMMENTS: Realistically, this man suffered some most unpleasant wartime experiences. In addition to the persistent bombing in Belgium, he apparently was given a job on the grave detail where he was required to "dig up bodies." He stated that the V-2 bombs in Belgium came every "four or five minutes" for a period of about five months. It seems clear that the patient was suffering from acute anxiety, traumatic in origin, upon discharge from the service. It is unfortunate that he did not receive proper psychological treatment at that time, because his problems have now solidified into a serious and perhaps intractable chronic disorder reinforced by secondary gains.

It is difficult to view this patient at this time as other than disabled. The degree of somaticization of his anxiety at this point, and his complete lack of insight into the emotional components of his disorder suggests a fragile ego that is easily fragmented. His years of being unable to cope with problems, followed by failure after failure, have weakened his self-esteem immeasurably to the point that if he were put under stress at the present time without a "way out," he could easily become psychotic.

The decision to allow disability for this man will be a difficult one for the agency to make because one is confronted with the alternative, if he is allowed disability, of perpetuating and reinforcing the pattern that has become a way of life with him. The prognosis is very poor, on the other hand, as far as effectively changing his lifestyle through a treatment program. Should he be allowed disability, he is capable of managing his own funds.

A CASE OF NEUROTIC ADJUSTMENT TO A CHRONIC AILMENT

This case illustrates the importance of obtaining the patient's psychological history in understanding the current disability. The patient was a thirty-nine-year-old white female. The patient has a serious circulatory problem involving vascular insufficiency, the etiology of which is not clear. Nevertheless, there is fairly general agreement among cardiologists that she is suffering from a chronic, and possibly progressive, circulatory disorder. The patient has been warned by at least one physician that she should avoid any strenuous activity of any type. Others have warned her that she should definitely curtail her activities.

Paradoxically perhaps, the patient has refused to accept the fact of her disabling illness. The medical director at the industry where she was employed recommended that she stop working and apply for disability insurance. The patient was reluctant to do so, and returned to the job several times, getting ill each time. Her persistent attempts to return to work finally prompted the medical director to refer her to a mental examiner for disability evaluation.

CLINICAL INTERVIEW: The patient was found to be a rather plainlooking, dark-haired woman who appeared somewhat older than her stated age. She was accompanied to the office by her husband. She stated her problem as follow: "If I get too tired or exhausted my blood pressure drops. I get faint, dizzy, exhausted, and sometimes black out. The doctors tell me my heart is not strong enough to push the blood through the veins. I've had this condition six to eight years and it has gradually gotten worse."

At times she had suffered such exhaustion that she was unable to drive her car home. At other times she has had to have her family help her into bed because of exhaustion. On occasion she has stayed in bed for as long as two weeks to get her strength back. She is treated medically by her physician with pills, and transfusions to increase her blood volume.

In regard to her condition, the patient stated, "I can't believe it. I don't want to believe it, I mean. I've always felt that I could move mountains. I can't stand being sick and being taken care of. My doctor tells me I'm slowly committing suicide, but still I can't seem to stop myself."

The patient thought that perhaps it all began several years ago when she ran out into the yard to meet her husband and suddenly "blacked out" which was preceded by intense chest pain. At that time she was told by her doctor that she had had a "heart attack."

The patient is an only child whose mother died when she was six weeks of age. She was given to her paternal grandmother and two maiden aunts to raise. Her father did not remarry until the patient was an adult. When questioned about her childhood years, the patient noted that she remembers acute feelings of being unwanted and being a "burden" on her grandmother and her aunts. She was told by her father many times that she was the reason that he never married again, and that he not feel "free" to marry as long as she was a burden to him. Her grandmother and aunts, according to the patient's memory, never let the patient forget that they were doing her a favor by raising her.

The patient's way of handling this was to do everything possible to make herself less of a burden to the family by throwing herself into hard work and into efforts to please other people. Being "sick" as a child was also a burden to them, and consequently she never felt that she had a right to be ill. Rather, to avoid the dreaded rejection she felt it necessary to work very hard, be very active, and make efforts to please everyone.

This type of adjustment worked fairly well for her, and when she finished high school successfully with average grades, she married a neighborhood boy and had three children. She continued her behavior of working very hard and always made it a point to "do" for other people. She also has always loved physical work of all kinds, in the yard or garden or around the house. Any kind of physical activity has been very gratifying to her, such as hiking in the mountains or fishing. The patient probably could have gone along this way for the rest of her life if she had not fallen ill physically. This exacerbated her underlying dependency problems and fears of rejection which may well have remained dormant had she not fallen ill.

As she expressed it, "I just can't adjust to other people doing things for me. I can't stand to not be up and going. I would rather be dead than have my family take care of me. I get terribly depressed if there's anything I'm not able to do."

She gets very depressed when she is in bed ill. At these times she feels that "one big hurt for her family (her death) would be better than a lot of small hurts (her up's and down's)," and at these times she thinks about suicide but states she would not consider it seriously.

In general, the patient has used massive denial between spells of illness. Thusly, when she is feeling well again she immediately throws herself into her old activities with no temperance or moderation. As a result she soon finds herself flat on her back again and dangerously ill. Of this she said, "When I'm not sick I can't believe that there's anything wrong with me. I refuse to believe it. I think it's all gone away now and that it will never come back again. My doctor has scolded with me and pleaded with me to no avail."

The patient has been happily married for twenty years, and has three teenage children. Since she has stopped her employment, her life has more than ever centered around her family. Her husband is a mild-mannered, easygoing and rather passive man who looks to his wife to lead the family in matters of activities and recreation. She plans picnics to the mountains on the weekends, the family goes to church together, and she spends her days washing and ironing and picking up the house. The family has friends and socializes.

This lifestyle continued until the patient got ill, which usually occurred rather suddenly, often with a "blackout spell." Her physician was called and he would hospitalize her on occasion or on other occasions treat her at home. He gives her medication to increase blood pressure, a diuretic, and I.V. infusions of glucose to increase her blood volume. She would rest in bed several days, and then throw herself back into the same activities.

MENTAL STATUS EXAMINATION: Mental status examination reveals an essentially "normal" woman. She was oriented in all spheres, had no problem with memory or concentration, was abstract in her thinking, but did suffer occasional bouts of mild to moderate depression related to her physical illness.

Bender-Gestalt reproductions revealed no visual-motor disorder. Rorschach results were characterized by a certain amount of denial, equivocation, and indecision. Considerable underlying depression was apparent in the content of her responses which seemed to be related to early maternal deprivation. Considerable bodily preoccupation was also apparent in the Rorschach, perhaps understandable considering her serious illness. There was no evidence of psychosis and reality testing was within normal limits.

Considering the amount of underlying depression seen on the Rorschach, we can assume that the life she has lived and her characterological adjustments are counterdepressive in nature. Apparently this is her way of handling the underlying depression, and for her it has been satisfactory most of her life—that is, until she became physically ill and could no longer utilize the mechanisms that previously served her well.

DIAGNOSTIC IMPRESSION: The patient suffers from depression secondary to her physical illness. When she feels well, she utilizes neurotic denial of her illness and throws herself into activities that literally threaten her life.

COMMENTS: Following the examination, I spent some time discussing these matters with the patient. I pointed out to her her repetition of an old pattern from childhood. That is, that she is still fighting her fear of rejection by making herself so important to her family that she feels assured of being wanted, needed, and loved. The patient was "stunned" by this interpretation, and had never related her handling of her illness to her childhood. She was able to use this information relatively constructively, and expressed the thought that this was a terribly important idea to her and that she would need to think about it a great deal.

I informed her that it was likely she could use some continued help in this regard, and suggested to her that if she could not afford private psychiatric care with this problem, she might apply for help at a local mental health center. She protested that they could not afford private help, or in fact could not afford to spend any money on this problem, and I then pointed out to her that she was doing the same thing again—namely, making sure she was not a financial "burden" to her husband and family. She then laughed and said that over the years her husband has literally begged her to spend money on herself and to buy things for herself, but she has never been able to do so.

Regarding the question of disability, this patient is disabled in the sense that she is handling her illness in a nonadaptive neurotic fashion. Assuming that she is physically capable of doing some work, I see her as emotionally or mentally disabled because she is unable to limit her activities in line with the realities of her illness. However, to pension her for this type of disability would be to create an iatrogenic illness if she is not given psychotherapy or counseling along with it.

In reality, her "psychological problem" is her physical illness, i.e. her fear of it, and her maladaptive efforts to cope with it.

A psychiatrist might be the therapist of choice in a case such as this because of his medical background. It will be necessary for him to work with the patient's physician. If she can receive therapeutic assistance in managing her illness, it would seem appropriate to believe that she is not completely disabled by any means. She could work productively, although at a slower pace.

I would recommend considering the patient disabled for a limited period of time, during which she and her husband should be urged to obtain psychiatric help for her to enable her to manage her illness. To judge her completely disabled would be to encourage the dependency which is so frightening to her, and would literally make her more ill.

With the approval of her psychiatrist, her disability might be withdrawn and referral made to vocational rehabilitation to help her find employment that is not strenuous or dangerous to her health.

Certain iatrogenic features seem possible in this case, pointing up the need for careful handling based on understanding the patient's emotional makeup. Her physician's recommendations that she stop work have frightened the patient into even more frantic activities, leading to a vicious cycle of repeated spells of illness and repeated warnings to stop work. This has resulted in a "snowball" effect of progressive exacerbation of her illness.

A CASE OF MENTAL DEFICIENCY

This case illustrates the importance of interviews with collaterals, in this case the patient's mother, in obtaining information about the patient. It also illustrates how the examiner can be helpful to the family in addition to diagnosing disability. The patient was eligible for disability benefits through a governmental agency.

CLINICAL INTERVIEW: The patient, a thirty-six-year-old white male, was brought to the office by his mother. He was found to be a tall, well-developed man dressed in laborer's clothes. His head above the ears seemed smaller than average, possibly borderline microcephalic.

When asked, he stated that his father had been dead for about three years. His mother is employed. He has two brothers and one sister.

When asked what he does for a living, he stated, "I used to work but now I just mess around and go to the beer joint to talk to people." When asked why he stopped work, he stated that about three months previously he had hurt his back on a farm, trying to push a truck out of mudhole. He went to the doctor, was hospitalized, and put in traction for a period of time.

When asked who he worked for, he stated that he worked for his father but "she (meaning mother) sold it (the farm) so I went to another farm. I worked for my dad eighteen years." The patient went to a neighboring farm to ask for a job. He worked there almost a year, and it was there that he hurt his back. After getting out of the hospital, he decided that he did not want to return to the farm, although he could have, saying that "the owner didn't like me."

When asked about his duties on the farm, he stated that he scooped grain, moved bales of hay to a feeding area, drove a pickup truck doing general odd jobs, and helped with sheep-shearing. These were the things he had done on his father's farm.

When asked about school experience, he stated that he had graduated from high school in regular classes and did "pretty well." He admitted he flunked one grade in elementary school.

When asked about siblings, he stated that they all lived away from home. Two of them were in jobs requiring a college education.

When asked if he was looking for a job, he stated that he had two jobs "lined up," and was only waiting for a telephone call to get started.

By this point in the interview, the examiner was puzzled as to why the patient was applying for disability benefits. He had said he worked many years successfully on his father's farm, that he had also worked at a neighbor's farm after the death of his father, that he could return there if he wished, that he had graduated from high school in regular classes and did "pretty well." He also stated that he had two jobs "lined up" with the implication that it was merely a matter of time before he got to work again.

The examiner asked the patient his understanding of why he was being examined. He stated that he did not know, but that his mother brought him here after talking to some men.

When asked how he spends his time when he is not working, the patient stated that he enjoyed going to various athletic events with friends of his. They would go to football, basketball, and baseball games, rodeos, wrestling matches, and sometimes to the movies. He and his mother go to church regularly.

When asked what his doctor had told him about his back, he stated that the doctor said he should not lift anything over fifty pounds. He did not have an operation in the hospital, bed rest and traction only.

When asked about his father's death three years previously, the patient got tears in his eyes and said he "took it pretty hard. We were pretty close. I got over it though."

INTERVIEW WITH COLLATERAL (PATIENT'S MOTHER): An interview with the patient's mother clarified the history considerably. She stated that she had had a very difficult labor with him, over fifty hours in duration, and he was at last "taken" by forceps. He had a badly scarred and bruised head. He was slow in walking and talking, and could not learn to ride a bicycle for many years.

In school, he was only "passed along" by his teachers which was the custom in small rural schools. When he was in high school she had him tutored for two years, which enabled him to learn to read.

Her other children were all mentally "normal" and went on to higher education. They are all interested in helping the patient as much as possible.

Around the farm, the patient had worked very closely with his father. She stated that he needed constant supervision, and needed to be told what to do. His father had taken him with him on the farm since he was a small boy. He had taught the patient simple duties to perform, which the patient could do in a repetitious fashion. Emotionally, the patient seemed fairly well adjusted while his father was alive, and he was always treated as a "man" by the family members and had a sense of self-respect.

After her husband died, the patient's mother was no longer able to keep the farm, and about two years later she sold it. As she spoke of her husband's death, she got tears in her eyes. She stated, "I know I should be over it, but I'm not." When asked how the patient adjusted to his father's death, his mother replied that he was very shaken up by it. They talked about it for a few days afterwards, but the mother then felt that the best thing for the patient was to not talk about it. When the patient brought up memories of his father, the mother was inclined to not answer or to say, "That was a long time ago." She felt that this was in the best interest of the patient, but it seemed by her tearful behavior during the interview that she herself had never coped with the fact of her husband's death.

When asked about her son's working experience since she sold the farm, she stated that a neighbor allowed him to work there only because he was "good-hearted." After the patient hurt his back, the neighbor took on a hired hand to replace him.

She said her son then applied for a variety of jobs "in town." As she put it, he has tried and tried but no one will hire him. She helped him fill out application forms because he could not read them. She stated that it was characteristic of him to tell acquaintances that he was "waiting for a phone call" about a job, implying that he was only temporarily unemployed. She has tried to encourage him to seek farm work since that is what he knows best. However, the patient has adamantly refused to return to the farm. He states the he wants an "inside job" such as a store clerk or factory work.

She thinks of the patient as "mildly retarded" and believes that if only the right job is found he will be able to live a relatively normal life.

PSYCHOLOGICAL TESTING: Psychological testing was used with this patient instead of a mental status exam, although many of the same conclusions could have been arrived at through mental status testing.

The Wechsler Adult Intelligence Scale was administered. On the Verbal Scale he obtained an IQ of 69, on the Performance Scale an IQ of 59, and a Full Scale IQ of 65. Subtest scores were all relatively consistent at a mentally defective level.

On the Verbal Scale, the patient did not know who Longfellow was, he thought there were 365 weeks in one year, and he thought that Brazil was located in Australia. He could not answer the question, "Why do we have to pay taxes," or give a meaning to the proverb "Strike while the iron is hot." On similarities, a dog and a lion "are not alike—one is big and one is little, and north and west "are different directions." In arithmetic, he did not know the total amount of six quarters, how many inches there are in two and one-half feet, or how many oranges one could buy for 36¢ if each orange cost 6¢. He was able to recite five digits forward but only two backward. On vocabulary he could not define the words fabric, assemble, conceal, enormous, or hasten.

On the Performance Scale, on a test involving identifying the missing parts in pictures, he was able to identify correctly only four out of twenty-one. On the block designs test, he got partial credit for the simplest block design, no credit for the next most difficult, got the third design correctly, but no more. As an experiment, the examiner tried to teach the patient how to work the block designs correctly. Even with tutoring, he was unable to get them correctly. In assembling objects (like jigsaw puzzles), the patient was able to get one correct out of four, and one partially correct. Other performance tests were accomplished at about the same level.

On the Bender-Gestalt Test, figure reproductions demonstrated severe distortions in reproduction, some of the reproductions almost unrecognizable.

On the Wide Range Achievement Test, the patient was able to read words at a sixth grade level, but his understanding of the words he read was at a third grade level. His score on the arithmetic test was at a kindergarten level. He could do only simple one-digit addition and subtraction.

DIAGNOSTIC IMPRESSION: Mental deficiency, moderate.

COMMENTS: Certainly this patient is disabled in the sense of expecting him to find significantly gainful employment and financial independence. He was employed full time for eighteen years only because he worked for his father, who made allowances for his handicap. Neither the patient nor his relatives have adjusted their expectations of the patient in line with the severity of his mental deficiency.

Although the patient will probably be declared eligible for disability allowance, he is not the kind of man who could be happy unemployed. He has been a productive person most of his life, and accepted by others on that basis, although his work was highly routinized and closely supervised.

The most logical place for the patient to work would be around a farm. It seems apparent, however, that the reason he no longer cares for that type of work is because it reminds him of his father, whose loss has never been resolved by the patient.

An appointment was made with the patient's mother and brother to discuss these matters, and several suggestions were made by the examiner. It was suggested that it is really not in the patient's best interest to refrain from talking about his deceased father. If he were encouraged to talk about his father, it is possible he might be willing to return to farm work someday.

Secondly, the loss of his father represented more than losing a loved person. Perhaps even more importantly, it was the loss of a sense of stability, direction, a "compass point" around which his working life revolved. This was very important to the patient because he is not capable of self-initiated and self-directed work. This leads us to the understanding that to simply find a job for the patient is not enough. As important is the necessity to find a man who is sensitive to the patient's needs in this regard and is willing to take that role with the patient.

Also discussed with the family was the degree of the patient's handicap. The mother had described him as "mildly retarded." The examiner explained the type of work that the patient might be expected to do under supervision, e.g. mow lawns, and the type he could not be expected to do, e.g. filling station attendant, store clerk, or security guard.

The patient's brother accepted the job of talking to some potential employers and exploring their interest in providing employment. Naturally, the patient could not expect the compensation that would be paid the usual employee.

The patient is not capable of managing his own funds. Probably his mother or brother would accept this responsibility.

SELECTED BIBLIOGRAPHY

1. Allison, J., Blatt, S.J., and Zimet, C.N. *The Interpretation of Psychological Tests*. New York, Harper and Row, 1968.
2. Anon.
3. Arieti, S. (Ed.): *American Handbook of Psychiatry*. New York, Basic Books, 1959, vols. I and II.
4. ———: Schizophrenia: the manifest symptomatology, the psychodynamic and formal mechanisms. In Arieti, S. (Ed.): *America Handbook of Psychiatry*. New York, Basic Books, 1959, vol. I.
5. Belmot, I., and Birch, H.G.: "Productivity" and mode of function in the Rorschach responses of brain damaged patients. *J Nerv Ment Dis, 134:* 1962.
6. Bender, L.: Bender visual motor gestalt test. In *The Psychological Corp Test Catalog*, New York, 1974.
7. Birch, H.G., and Diller, L.; Rorschach signs of "organicity": a physiological basis for perceptual disturbances. *J Proj Tech, 23:* 1959.
8. Brodsky, C.: Social psychiatric consequences of job incompetence. *Comprehen Psychiat, 12:6,* 1971.
9. Burgermeister, B.B.: *Psychological Techniques in Neurological Diagnosis*. New York, Hoeber Med. Div., Harper and Row, 1962.
10. Chrzanowski, G.: Neurasthenia and hypochondriasis. In Arieti, S. (Ed.): *American Handbook of Psychiatry*. New York, Basic Books, 1959, vol. I.
11. Conant, D., Assistant Supervisor, Disability Determination Unit, Social Security Administration, Denver office. Personal communication, 1973.
12. Danesino, A., and Shatin, L.: Occupational psychiatry in the United States: evolution and current trends. *Ann Freniatria Scienze Affini,* 79:2, 1966.
13. Diagnostic patterns in disability: Colorado and the nation. (Mimeo.) Chief Medical Consultant, State of Colorado Social Security Disability Determination Unit, 1970.
14. *Disability Evaluation under Social Security: A Handbook for Physicians.* U.S. Government Printing Office, 1970. 0–389–829.
15. Eadie, M.J.: Some aspects of episodic giddiness. *Med J Aust,* 2:11, 1968.
16. Flor-Henry, P.: Schizophrenic-like reactions and affective psychoses

associated with temporal lobe epilepsy: etiological factors. *Am J Psychiat, 126:3,* 1969.

17. Garrett, E.S., et al.: Diagnostic testing for cortical brain impairment. *Arch Neurol Psychiat, 77:* 1957.
18. Garrett, J. F.: *Psychological Aspects of Physical Disability.* U.S. Dept. of Health, Education, and Welfare, Office of Voc. Rehab., Washington, D.C., 1952.
19. Gibbert, F. B.: Epilepsy. *Brit Med J, 4:* 1969.
20. Goldstein, K.: Functional disturbances in brain damage. In Arieti, S. (Ed.): *American Handbook of Psychiatry.* New York, Basic Books, 1959, vol. I.
21. ———: The effect of brain damage on the personality. *Psychiatry, 15:* 1952.
22. Goldstein, K., and Scheener, M.: Abstract and concrete behavior: an experimental study with special tests. *Psychol Monogr, 53:* 1941.
23. Greenberg, I. M.: Cerebral dysfunction in general psychiatric office practice patients. Xerox, 1970.
24. Heimburger, R. F., and Reitan, R. M.: Easily administered written test for lateralizing brain lesions. *J Neurosurg, 18:* 1961.
25. Joynt, R. T., et al.: Behavioral and pathological correlates of motor impersistence. *Neurology, 12:* 1962.
26. Kardiner, A.: *The Traumatic Neuroses of War.* New York, Hoeber, 1941.
27. Kennard, M.: Value of equivocal signs in neurological diagnosis. *Neurology, 10:* 1960.
28. Klebanoff, S. G., et al: Psychological consequences of brain lesions and ablations. *Psychol Bull, 51:1,* 1954.
29. Klein, R. J.: The wages of disability. *Money, 3:4,* 1974.
30. Klopfer, B. (Ed.): *Developments in the Rorschach Technique, II.* Yonkers, New York, World Book, 1952.
31. Knights, R. M., and Hinton, G. G.: Minimal brain dysfunction: clinical and psychological test characteristics. *Acad Ther, 4:* 1969.
32. Ladd, C. E.: WAIS performance of brain damaged and neurotic patients. *J Clin Psychol, 20:* 1964.
33. Lansdell, H.: A general intellectual factor affected by temporal lobe dysfunction. *J Clin Psychol, 27:* 1971.
34. Lead poison study finds blacks suffer at rate 3 times whites. Reported anon: *New York Times,* Dec. 7, 1971.
35. Ludwig, E. G., and Collette, J.: Dependency, social isolation and mental health in a disabled population. *Soc Psychiat, 5:2,* 1970.
36. Luria, A. F.: *Higher Cortical Functions in Man.* New York, Basic Books, 1966.

37. McDaniel, J. W.: *Physical Disability and Human Behavior.* New York, Pergamon Press, 1969.

38. McFie, J.: Psychological testing in clinical neurology. *J Nerv Ment Dis, 131:* 1960.

39. Meier, M. J., and Resch, J. A.: Behavioral prediction of short-term neurologic change following acute onset of cerbrovascular symtoms. *Mayo Clinic Proc, 1967.*

40. *Methodical Assessment of Psychiatric Impairment.* U.S. Dept. of Health, Education, and Welfare, Social Security Administration, July, 1970. SS PUB NO. 43–70(7–70).

41. Morgan, D. H.: Neuro-psychiatric problems of cardiac surgery. *J Psychosom Res, 15:* 1971.

42. Nielsen, J. M.: *Agnosia, Apraxia, Aphasia: Their Value in Cerebral Localization.* New York, Hafner, 1962.

43. ————: *A Textbook of Clinical Neurology,* 3rd ed. New York, Hoeber, 1962.

44. Nussbaum, K., et al.: Psychiatric assessment in the Social Security program of disability insurance. *Am J Psychiat, 126:6,* 1969.

45. ————: Psychiatric disability rating in transition. *Compr Psychiatry, 10:4,* 1969.

46. ————: Psychiatric evidence needed in Social Security disability evaluation. *J Indiana Med Assoc, 61:* 1968.

47. ————: Psychological assessment in the Social Security program of disability insurance. *Am Psychol, 24:* 1969.

48. Organic Conditions (authored variously). In Arieti, S. (Ed.): *American Handbook of Psychiatry.* New York, Basic Books, vol. I.

49. Papp, A.: Psychological investigation of the relation between the period of sickpay and regaining working capacity. *Pszichological Tanulmanyok, 8:* 1965.

50. Parsons, O. A., and Vega, A.: Different psychological effects of lateralized brain damage. *J Consult Clin Psychol, 33:5,* 1969.

51. Piotrowski, Z.: The Rorschach ink-blot method in organic disturbance of the central nervous system. *J Nerv Ment Dis, 86:* 1937.

52. Popick, B.: What the Social Security disability program means to you and your patients. *Metabolism, 12:00,* 1968.

53. Portnoy, I.: The anxiety state. In Arieti, S. (Ed.): *American Handbook of Psychiatry.* New York, Basic Books, vol. I.

54. Pribram, K. H.: *Languages of the Brain: Experimental Paradoxes and Principles in Neuropsychology.* Englewood Cliffs, N.J., Prentice-Hall, 1971.

55. Reitan, R. M.: Psychological assessment of deficits associated with brain lesions in subjects with normal and subnormal intelligence. In Khanna, J. L. (Ed.): *Brain Damage and Mental Retardation: A Psychological Evaluation.* Springfield, Thomas, 1967.

56. ———: Psychological deficits resulting from cerebral lesions in man. In Warren, J. M., and Akert, K. (Eds.): *Pre-frontal Granular Cortex and Behavior.* New York, McGraw Hill, 1964.

57. ———: The effects of brain lesions on adaptive abilities in human beings. Indianapolis, Indiana, Indiana University Medical Center, 1959. Mimeo.

58. ———: The validity of the Trail Making Test as an indicator of organic brain damage. *Percept Mot Skills, 8:* 1958.

59. ———: Trail Making Test, Manual for Administration, Scoring, and Interpretation (Mimeo). Ordered from R. Reitan, 7708 89th Place S.E., Wash., Mercer Island.

60. Rochford, J. M., et al.: Neuropsychological impairments in functional psychiatric diseases. *Arch Gen Psychiatry, 22:* 1970.

61. Schafer, R.: *Psychoanalytic Interpretation in Rorschach Testing.* New York, Grune and Stratton, 1970.

62. Schmideberg, M.: The borderline patient. In Arieti, S. (Ed.): *American Handbook of Psychiatry.* New York, Basic Books, vol. I.

63. Selye, H.: *Stress of Life.* New York, McGraw-Hill, 1956.

64. Shaffer, J. W., et al.: MMPI profiles of disability insurance claimants. *Amer J Psychiatry, 129:4,* 1972.

65. ———: Psychiatric assessment from documentary evidence. *Compr Psychiatry, 12:*00–00, 1971.

66. Small, L.: *Neuropsychodiagnosis in Psychotherapy.* New York, Bruner/Mazel, 1973.

67. Stevenson, I.: The psychiatric interview. In Arieti, S. (Ed.): *American Handbook of Psychiatry.* New York, Basic Books, vol. I, 1959.

68. Stevenson, I., and Sheppe, W. M., Jr.: The psychiatric examination. In Arieti, S. (Ed.): *American Handbook of Psychiatry.* New York, Basic Books, 1959, vol. I.

69. Surridge, D.: An investigation into some psychiatric aspects of multiple sclerosis. *Br J Psychiatry, 115:* 1969.

70. Tauber, L. E.: Man's humanity to man: A proposed change in the world insurance created. *Ontario Psychologist, 3:*6, 1971.

71. Tyner, J. H., and Sutherland, J. M.: *Exercises in Neurological Diagnosis.* Edinburgh and London, Churchill Livingston, 1972.

72. Volle, F. O.: A proposal for "testing the limits" with mental defectives for purposes of subtest analysis of the WISC verbal scale. *J Clin Psychol, 13:*1, 1957.

73. Walker, Sydney, III: *Psychiatric Signs and Symptoms due to Medical Problems.* Springfield, Thomas, 1967.

74. Wechsler, D.: *The Measurement and Appraisal of Adult Intelligence.* Baltimore, Williams and Wilkins, 1958.

75. ———: Wechsler Adult Intelligence Scale. In *The Psychological Corporation Test Catalog.* New York, 1974.

76. Wechsler, D., and Stone, C.: *Wechsler Memory Scale*. New York, Psychological Corp. Test Catalog, 1974.
77. Whitten, J. R.: Psychical Seizures. *Am J Psychiatry, 126:*4, 1969.
78. Wilson, W. P.: How an EEG helped solve a diagnostic puzzle of anxiety. Reported anon, *Frontiers of Psychiatry*, May, 1972.
79. Zimet, C. N., and Fishman, D. B.: Psychological deficit in schizophrenia and brain damage. *Ann Rev Psychol, 21:* 1970.
80. Zivin, I.: The neurological and psychiatric aspects of hypoglycemia. *Dis Nerv Syst,* 3:19, 1970.

INDEX

117